THE ULTIMATE BOOK OF
MARTIAL ARTS

FAY GOODMAN

HERMES
HOUSE

This edition is published by Hermes House,
an imprint of Anness Publishing Ltd,
Hermes House, 88–89 Blackfriars Road, London SE1 8HA;
tel. 020 7401 2077; fax 020 7633 9499
www.hermeshouse.com; www.annesspublishing.com

If you like the images in this book and would like to investigate using them for
publishing, promotions or advertising, please visit our website www.practicalpictures.com
for more information.

Publisher: JOANNA LORENZ
Project Editors: ALISON MACFARLANE, HELEN WILSON & ZOE ANTONIOU
Designer: LISA TAI
Photographer: MIKE JAMES

ETHICAL TRADING POLICY

Because of our ongoing ecological investment programme, you, as our customer,
can have the pleasure and reassurance of knowing that a tree is being cultivated on your
behalf to naturally replace the materials used to make the book you are holding.
For further information about this scheme, go to www.annesspublishing

PUBLISHER'S NOTE

The author and publishers have made every effort to ensure that all instructions contained
within this book are accurate and safe, and cannot accept liability for any resulting injury,
damage or loss to persons or property, however it may arise. If you do have any special needs
or problems, consult your doctor or another health professional. This book cannot replace
medical consultation and should be used in conjunction with professional advice. You should
not attempt martial arts without training from a properly qualified practitioner.

THANK YOU

To those who have been kind – thank you
To those who have believed – I am grateful
To those who are sincere – you are deep in my thoughts
So let us never despair
When all appears against us
And the evil ones try to take our heart and soul
For those of you who have believed and never faltered
This is what living is made worthwhile for – I thank you

Fay Goodman

CONTENTS

INTRODUCTION

There are millions of martial arts practitioners all over the world. Through the disciplines these arts impose, men, women and children of all ages and abilities are actively involved in learning how to improve their awareness, health, fitness, confidence and their ability to protect themselves.

The popular perception – learned largely from movies and fictional television dramas – that martial arts are mainly concerned with violence and general mayhem, has done much harm by discouraging people from achieving a more in-depth understanding. Anyone who becomes involved with the martial arts soon learns that the aggressive, brutish perception people have of these disciplines could not be further from the truth. Inherent in their teaching are the guiding principles of respect, courtesy and self-discipline – in fact, most skilled martial arts practitioners are less likely to initiate or become involved in physical aggression than non-practitioners, preferring instead to remove themselves from a potentially violent situation. Rather than fighting other people, the martial arts encourage us to fight the enemy within in an effort to become better people. Combine this attitude with the inner strength one gains from their training, and the rewards to be gleaned are peace of mind and a richer, more rounded quality of life.

While some arts may, superficially, appear to be aggressive, especially when weapons are used, this is far from their true meaning. The use of the sword, for example, in its

Although the popular conception of many martial arts is one of physical aggression, this is far from the reality which demands respect, courtesy and self-discipline.

The study of the philosophy of Shinto lies behind most martial arts disciplines.

philosophy and teachings, is concerned with developing your mind and body to work harmoniously together and, if you relate this to self-protection, it is about having the confidence and ability to be aware of a confrontation before it happens. This enables you, if you are threatened, to have the courage to walk or talk your way out of a difficult situation without resorting to physical confrontation. In nearly every situation, the price of violence is too high to pay. In the words of Musashi Miyamoto, one of Japan's most famous swordsmen (1584-1645): "We need to win the battle before we enter and in many ways we should never need to draw our sword."

About this book

The aim of this book is to give you an insight into a selection of martial arts commonly practised throughout the world today. While some of the chapters give step-by-step instruction on how to practise some of the basic moves of the

Courtesy is the foundation of martial arts. This two-handed gesture used before and after training denotes sincerity and respect.

The essence of judo is the utilization of your opponent's body weight as well as your own.

Zokin-training (floor rag cleaning). This ego-less act is symbolically one of purification, preparation and discipline.

chosen discipline, there can be no substitute for learning from a professionally recognized, experienced and highly skilled teacher, who will instruct and assist you in the development of your chosen art. It is important that you train in a safe environment, that you are aware of emergency procedures in case of accidents, and that you have proper insurance cover.

Within the chapters you will find a brief overview of each martial art's history and philosophy and the essential clothing and equipment you need in order to take part. Etiquette, warm-up exercises and basic techniques are also included, as well as an insight into some of the weaponry that is traditionally used. Some of the techniques are for demonstration purposes only, designed to give you an idea as to what the chosen art has to offer in terms of stances, postures and the use of weapons, if any.

If you are a more experienced martial arts practitioner, this book may introduce you to disciplines that you have not yet explored. It is very common for practitioners to study more than one art – the chief difficulty usually lies in deciding which others would be most beneficial. The wide-ranging view given here of the different philosophies and

Tai chi chuan is enjoyed by men and women of all ages.

A young girl demonstrating the skill and precision required in karate.
Good instruction is vital when learning a martial art at any age.

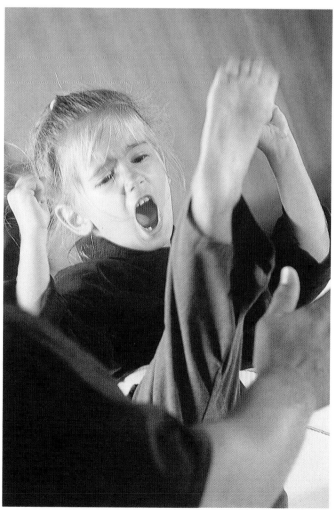

skills, and an appreciation of what each discipline has to offer, along with the benefits, will hopefully assist you in making the best decision.

Throughout this book, references will be made to the training area, which is known as the *dojo.* This term is very common in the martial arts and was first used in kenjutsu – now more commonly known as kendo. There are a variety of spellings of some of the martial art disciplines featured in this book. I have attempted to use the most common spelling and format. Be aware that you may see the names spelt differently, where for example, ju-jitsu can also be spelt ju-jutsu or jiu-jitsu. The same can be said of tae kwondo which is also commonly referred to as tac-kwondo.

I hope that you will enjoy using this book and that you will learn at least a little about the many wonderful and varied martial arts, as well as something of the teachers throughout the ages who have left us with the legacy of skills that we can now enjoy today. The world of the martial arts has many doors, and, in the words of one famous Chinese proverb: "Teachers open the door but we must walk through by ourselves."

TAE KWONDO

태
권
도

It is widely believed that a Buddhist monk named Won Qwang originated the five principles – etiquette, modesty, perseverance, self-control and indomitable (invincible) spirit – that today form the basis of tae kwondo. This art is renowned for its exceptional kicking and jumping techniques. It is viewed not only as an extremely effective self-defence system, but is also a very popular international sport. Early training involves simple punching and blocking techniques, which many may also relate to karate.

TAE KWONDO

태
권
도

history *and* philosophy

Tae kwondo is derived from several martial arts, with the main influence being tae-kyon – Korean kick fighting. *Tae* means "to kick" or "smash with the feet"; *kwon* means "to intercept" or "strike with the hands"; and *do* means "the way of the art". Thus, the foundation of the art is the use of the hands and feet to overcome an attacker swiftly.

Tae kwondo was originally developed in Korea in the 1950s, when a group of leading martial arts experts came together to unify their respective disciplines under a single fighting system. The inauguration took place in South

Korea on 11 April, 1955, with Major-General Choi Hong Hi, a 9th-*dan* black belt, being credited as the founder. However, its roots stretch back nearly 2,000 years, when it was born from an art known as *hwarang do*, meaning "the way of the flowering manhood".

The *hwarang* were young noblemen, influenced by Confucian teachings, who formed a patriotic society during the unification of Korea, in the Silla dynasty, in about AD600. The Silla kingdom was the smallest of three within the Korean peninsula, and was constantly under attack from

The instructor demonstrates the flexibility and balance required by a kick to the head.

A scissor kick in tae kwondo, which is based upon ancient Korean martial arts.

its two stronger neighbours. It was these constant invasions that led the Silla nobility to develop a fighting system to protect their kingdom.

Towards the end of the 10th century, following the unification of Korea, learning tae kwondo became compulsory for all young men. However, in about the 16th century the military traditions of the country fell out of general favour and the practice of tae kwondo was kept alive only by Buddhist monks. Following the Japanese occupation in 1909, the suppression of any form of martial art only served to further its decline. The few remaining dedicated practitioners emigrated to China and Japan and, thus, the art survived.

Following liberation in 1945, many Korean exiles returned to their homeland and reintroduced an improved version of tae kwondo. The Korean government, as part of its campaign to reassert national identity following years of Japanese occupation, supported the practice of tae kwondo by officially sponsoring it. This led to a more formal approach to the teaching and grading of the discipline.

Tae kwondo spread worldwide from Korea in the 1960s, and the first World Tae Kwondo Championship took place in Seoul, South Korea, in 1973. Since 1988, tae kwondo has been listed as an Olympic sport.

Competition fighting

Competition fighting in tae kwondo is purely optional. For those who participate, competitions are split into three sections: sparring, patterns and destruction.

Sparring involves two practitioners practising fighting techniques to develop their timing, focus and speed. It is performed in a controlled environment so that no unnecessary injuries occur. In competition, the aim is to score points through the delivery of correct techniques to target areas.

Patterns are a set series of combination techniques performed in a sequential order against an imaginary opponent. This is similar to karate, which refers to patterns as *kata*, or kung fu, which uses set movements called "forms". One of the first patterns a practitioner learns is *chon ji tul* (the heaven and earth pattern).

Destruction refers to "breaking techniques", in which practitioners learn to break, for example, a piece of wood. The aim is to ensure that the power and skill of the technique are truly effective. It is also designed to focus the mind.

BENEFITS OF TAE KWONDO

Learning tae kwondo can have benefits in many different aspects of your everyday life. These include:

- Health and fitness
- Flexibility and stamina
- Confidence and well-being
- Self-awareness and assertiveness
- Comradeship
- Self-defence skills
- Stress reduction
- Positive attitude
- Strength of character
- Discipline of mind and body

clothing *and*
equipment

Practitioners in tae kwondo require a plain white heavy weight cotton suit. This consists of a plain V-neck white jacket and trousers with elasticated waist. Instructors of 1st-*dan* and above wear a slightly different suit (*dobuk*) which has black edging around the neck. Higher grades, 4th-*dan* and above, wear a black stripe down the side of the trousers. It is important to ensure that the suit (*gi*) is the right size for a smart appearance and to feel comfortable when practising various techniques. Protective clothing is worn on occasions when this is deemed necessary by both men and women – and usually when free fighting (sparring) is taking place or a public demonstration. Clothing should always be kept clean and tidy.

Clothing needs to be clean, comfortable and durable for the many kicking techniques practised.

BELT GRADINGS

10th-*kup*	White
9th-*kup*	White with yellow stripe
8th-*kup*	Yellow
7th-*kup*	Yellow with green stripe
6th-*kup*	Green
5th-*kup*	Green with blue stripe
4th-*kup*	Blue
3rd-*kup*	Blue with red stripe
2nd-*kup*	Red
1st-*kup*	Red with black stripe
1st-*dan* and upwards	Black

A gold tag denotes the level achieved for *dan* gradings.

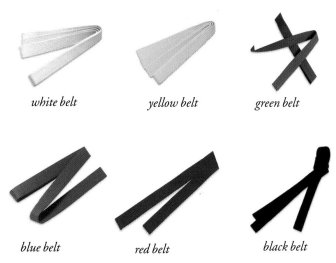

white belt   *yellow belt*   *green belt*

blue belt   *red belt*   *black belt*

Etiquette

There is only one bow performed in tae kwondo as part of etiquette and discipline. Practitioners perform a bow (*kyong ye*) upon entering the training area (*dojang*) as a sign of respect to the training environment. This bow is performed also to the instructor and students as a sign of respect prior to instruction or training.

1 ◁ Stand in a relaxed position, with your feet a shoulder-width apart, and your hands held behind your back.

2 ◁ Bring your open hands to the sides of your body and bring your feet together, with your heels touching and your toes slightly apart.

3 ▷ Bow, lowering your body approximately 30 degrees, with your eyes looking forwards.

Exercise | Warm-up

Tae kwondo specializes in leg techniques and the following exercises assist in gently stretching all the muscles and sinews required before practice. By correct stretching and toning of the whole body, we work towards minimizing any injury. The following depicts a selection of exercises to be found in tae kwondo, showing the flexibility which can be achieved.

WARM-UP 1 – *This exercise will stretch your legs, hamstrings and inner thighs.*

◁ Lower your body into a squatting position and push your left leg out to the side so that it is flat to the floor and with your toes pointing upwards. Clasp your hands in front of your body and try to maintain an upright posture. Repeat this exercise on the opposite side. This is not an easy exercise to perform in the early stages, so do not worry if you are unable to lower your leg as depicted. As long as your leg is kept straight, regular practice will enable you to become very supple.

WARM-UP 2 – *This is a hip-joint exercise.*

▷ While sitting on the floor, place your left leg across your right thigh. Place your right arm across your left knee and pull your left leg backwards. Ensure that your right heel is tucked well back towards your right thigh. Look in the opposite direction from your knee when levering your left leg backwards to cause a twisting action on your body. Repeat on the opposite side.

WARM-UP 3 – *Designed to stretch your legs and body generally, this exercise is particularly beneficial for your lower back and the backs of your legs.*

◁ Sit on the floor and pull your right heel into your groin area. Keep your left leg straight with your foot and toes pulled back. Lean forwards from the waist and grab your left foot with both hands. Try, if possible, to lower your head on to your knee, keeping your leg straight and flat to the floor. This may not be possible in the early stages but, with practice, you will eventually be able to achieve this position quite comfortably.

WARM-UP 4 – *This exercise is particularly useful for stretching your hamstrings, and increasing mobility of the hips, calf muscles and knee joints. Repeat this exercise to the right side. Again, the degree of flexibility may vary depending upon experience.*

❶ ◁ Sit on the floor and push your legs apart as far as you comfortably can. Take hold of your left ankle or foot with both hands and pull your body downwards towards your left knee. Try to touch your knee with your forehead. Bear in mind that it takes time for your muscles to become sufficiently supple to allow you to perform this exercise to its full extent. Hold this position for only a few seconds and repeat on the opposite side.

❷ ◁ With your legs still apart, take hold of both ankles. Lower your body as far as you can, with the aim of trying to touch the floor with your forehead. Hold this position for a few seconds only and do not worry if your head does not touch the floor, it is the actual lowering movement which stretches the relevant muscles and this must be built up gradually. Again, this is a very difficult exercise to perform if you are not extremely supple. Be patient – it may take months before you can fully achieve this movement.

WARM-UP 5 – *An important part of the warm-up routine is preparation for kicking.*

❶ ◁ With your partner turned away from you, place both of your hands on his shoulders for support. Swing your right leg sideways and as high as you can and repeat the exercise several times to loosen your thighs. Repeat the exercise with your left leg. Try to keep your leg as straight as possible.

❷ ▷ A similar exercise is to swing your leg, first forwards and then to the rear, while resting the side of your face on the top of your partner's back. Repeat this exercise several times with your right leg and then your left.

WARM-UP 6 – *Advanced exercise utilizing a partner to assist in stretching the inner thighs.*

CAUTION
This exercise must be performed only under professional supervision. Both partners must be well experienced and of similar weight and build.

◁ Sit on the floor and draw your feet in towards your groin, so that your knees are splayed out. Your partner, from the rear, gently places both hands on your shoulders for balance. He then carefully places his feet on your knees but does not, under any circumstances, bear down with all his weight on your knees. It is important that your partner maintains good balance and control as he gently pushes down on your knees. It is not the intention initially to bring your knees flat to the floor, as this could cause severe discomfort or even injury, but over a period of time you will come closer and closer to achieving this.

Technique | Basics

There are a variety of basic techniques in tae kwondo, of which the following demonstrates two blocks and strikes. These are designed to develop the skills required in tae kwondo and beginners need to practise slowly in the early stages. Speed will come in time, with practice.

BASIC TECHNIQUE 1 – *Lower parry block and spear hand strike to the chest.*

1 △ Face your partner in a formal stance with your right foot forward. Make sure that you have a good bend on your front knee and that your back leg is straight. Your partner adopts a left forwards stance, with his left leg forwards and right rear leg straight. Your partner then aims a punch at you with his left hand as he moves in towards you. Your response is a right-arm downwards palm block to prevent contact while you bring your left hand back, fingers straight and palm uppermost, in preparation to strike.

2 △ Strike your partner with your spear hand, aiming for your partner's solar plexus. Your thumbs should be tucked in and your fingers straight and locked together. Ensure that your right hand is under your left elbow to give support to the striking technique.

BASIC TECHNIQUE 2 – *Middle body block and ridge hand strike to temple.*

1 △ Remaining in the same stance, aim a punch towards your partner's solar plexus with your right fist. Your partner brings his left hand around in a semi-circle to deflect your attack.

2 △ Your partner then moves through to strike with the ridge of his right open hand to the side of your neck.

Technique | Self-defence for women

The following tae kwondo techniques are demonstrated as useful self-defence skills for women, although they are also applicable to men and children. The emphasis here is to develop confidence to handle an aggressive situation successfully by practising a strong stance, good posture and effective delivery of a technique.

SELF-DEFENCE 1 – *Elbow defence.*

❶ △ Face your partner. As she strikes at your solar plexus with a left fist, step back with your left leg into a back stance, with about 70 per cent of your body weight on your rear leg, and deflect the attack with a circular open-hand knife-edge block. Ensure that your thumb is tucked in and your fingers firmly pushed together. Simultaneously, bring your left fist back to your hip in preparation to deflect or strike, whichever is required.

❷ △ Step through with your right leg and strike with your right elbow to your partner's mandible.

△ Here you can clearly see the elbow strike to the mandible. Note the scream (*kiai*). This is an exhalation of air that tenses the body and enhances the delivery of the strike.

SELF-DEFENCE 2 – *Knee defence.*

❶ △ Your opponent comes at you from the front and attempts to apply a stranglehold. Step back with your left leg, keeping a good bend on your front knee and with your rear leg straight. Keep both your hands in and then move them outwards in a double open-hand wedge block to deflect the strike.

❷ △ Take hold of the back of your partner's head with both your hands and pull her face forwards and towards your left knee.

❸ △ The conclusion to this technique is a fully executed knee strike to your partner's head. Remember, be careful when practising these exercises and aim to focus your techniques at least 4 in (10 cm) away from your partner's head.

ADVANCED
Technique | Leg striking

The following is a selection of some of the superb leg-kicking techniques that are an integral part of tae kwondo. They are designed to strike the opponent from a variety of different angles and are particularly difficult for blocking. Tae kwondo uses a variety of sweeping, turning, spinning and jumping kicks as legs are a very powerful natural weapon.

TURNING KICK – *Using the ball of the foot to strike with an outwards, inwards kicking motion.*

1 △ With your left foot firmly planted on the floor, lift your right knee as high as you can to the side. Ensure that your fists are in a front guard position. Look directly at your opponent.

2 △ Bring your right leg around to the front in a circular movement as you fully extend it into a kick. The aim is to strike your opponent with the ball of the foot.

TWISTING KICK – *Using the ball of the foot to strike with an inwards, outwards kicking motion.*

◁ This is fundamentally a spinning kick to catch your opponent on the move. This technique requires a lot of practice to perfect into a proficient leg-striking technique. Note the unusual angle of the kick and the alignment of the body.

JUMPING SIDE KICK – *Using the side of the foot when elevated in order to strike.*

△ This is often viewed as one of the most spectacular of leg-striking techniques. Practitioners aim to reach great heights through constant training. A skilled practitioner, utilizing the jumping-side kick, can easily strike the face of a tall opponent.

DOWNWARD KICK, OR AXE KICK – *Using the heel to deliver a strong kick from a high raised position.*

◁ The aim of the axe kick is to raise your leg as high as possible, and then bring the heel down hard enough to break an opponent's collar bone.

Technique | Children's leg-strikes

This selection of tae kwondo self-defence techniques is suitable for children to practise. Note that in all cases the kick falls well short of actual body contact to maintain safety. It is important that children only practise those techniques which will enhance their well-being and not hinder their physical development.

FRONT KICK – Ap chagi.

△ Demonstrating the front kick, striking with the ball of the foot to an aggressor's solar plexus.

BACK HEEL KICK – Dwit chagi.

△ Demonstrating a back heel strike to the solar plexus area.

SIDE KICK – Yap chagi.

△ A side kick to the solar plexus area is an effective deterrent, giving a child time to get to a place of safety.

TURNING KICK – Dollya chagi.

△ The momentum of the side turn adds to the effectiveness of this leg-striking technique, which uses the ball of the foot to make contact.

Technique | Women in tae kwondo

Women can enjoy tae kwondo training for a number of reasons, and whilst the following leg techniques are demonstrated by women, they are also utilized by both men and children. Women, in particular, will find that being able to deliver such skilled leg techniques can enhance their health, fitness, confidence and self-defence skills.

JUMPING TURNING KICK – *Catching the opponent off guard by jumping and striking the face area which is difficult to block.*

▷ Demonstrating a jumping turning kick, aiming for an opponent's throat or face.

BACK KICK – *Demonstrating flexibility of kicking techniques when striking to the rear.*

▽ A back kick to an opponent's solar plexus. This is known as a short range back kick where the leg is kept bent. There are similar techniques where the rear kick requires the leg to push back and become straight.

SIDE KICK FROM THE FLOOR – *A good self-defence technique.*

▷ Here is a demonstration of self-defence from what seems to be a vulnerable position. The side kick from the floor aims for an opponent's solar plexus, but could be equally effective if delivered to the groin, knee or shin.

Technique | Kicking and breaking

The following demonstrates the skills that people, even those with major disabilities, can achieve. There are no barriers on the grounds of age, gender or ability, even though tae kwondo is viewed as a highly skilled leg-striking art. Dedication, discipline and persever- ance are the qualities required, along with comradeship amongst all practitioners.

CRESCENT KICK

△ A very complicated move, involving a back twist, spin and jump kick. This movement is achieved by swinging the leg in a crescent motion towards the target area.

SIDE KICK

△ This is a side kick to the head. Note the introduction of protective equipment. In tae kwondo practitioners are required to wear hand mitts, shin guards, feet protectors, gum shields (mouth guards), head guards and groin protection (athletic cup), along with any other necessary equipment, when performing sparring.

BACK-HOOK TECHNIQUE

△ Note the good posture and balance involved in this back-hook technique. The practitioner receiving the strike has complete confidence that the strike will be well focused and that no contact will be made.

TURNING KICK

△ Demonstrating a turning kick to the back of an opponent's head. Again, note the good posture and body guard and how the top of the foot is being used to deliver the strike. In a street-defence situation the instep of the foot could be used to strike. The ball of the foot can also be used when performing breaking techniques.

BREAKING TECHNIQUE

Caution: Do not practise this technique without strict professional supervision. Breaking techniques are for demonstration purposes only and they show the powerful leg techniques of the art. They can take years to perfect.

△The ball of the foot being used to perform a breaking technique.

KARATE

Karate is a self defence system that utilizes the whole of the human body and the ways in which it moves and twists. Techniques vary from punching and striking with the fist, hands and elbows, to kicks and strikes with the feet, shins and knees. As with many of the martial arts, karate is often seen by those who have no experience of it as a "killing art", but to true practitioners the opposite is, in fact, the case. Karate, whether practised as an art, sport or as self-defence, carries the motto "never strike the first blow".

空手

KARATE 空手

history *and* philosophy

Karate, or karate-do, loosely translated means "empty hand" (*kara* means "empty" and *te* means "hand"), and this art is indeed predominantly concerned with fighting with bare hands and feet. The basic principle is to turn the body into an effective weapon to defend and attack when and where it is appropriate.

Karate can be regarded as both a sport as well as a self-defence art depending on the emphasis of the club or association that is followed. Some instructors or coaches of karate place great emphasis on classical teachings, which incorporate traditional movements (such as *kata*) and philosophy, while others focus more on competition training. Some instructors, like Eugene Codrington, teach all aspects of the art. Karate is also an effective system of self-defence, which originally evolved on the Japanese island of Okinawa, where the carrying of weapons was forbidden, and so the inhabitants had to learn surreptitiously to protect themselves by other means.

Karate is one the most widely practised of the oriental martial arts. It evolved during one of the Japanese occupations of the island of Okinawa, part of the Ryukyu chain of islands, in the 15th century. Its roots, however, can be traced back much further than this – all the way back to ancient

A figure from the Shaolin Temple illustrates the connection between Okinawan karate, Japanese karate and weaponry.

Concentration, focus and intensity are essential qualities in competitive karate

India and China. Many people hold the view that what we today regard as the oriental martial arts have their roots in India. Indeed, when we look at such disciplines as yoga and the breathing techniques that originated in India, there does seem to be a great similarity between those and many of the modern martial arts systems.

It is believed that Zen Buddhist monks took the Indian fighting techniques to China from as early as the 5th and 6th centuries BC. Bodidharmi, the most famous of these monks, travelled at the end of the 5th century AD from India to China, where he became an instructor at the Shaolin monastery. He taught a combination of empty-hand fighting systems and yoga, and this became the well-known Shaolin kung fu – the system on which many Chinese martial arts systems are based.

In 1470, the Japanese had occupied the island of Okinawa. The law of the land dictated that anybody found carrying weapons would be put to death. In order to protect themselves from local bandits, who largely ignored the prohibition on weapons, Zen Buddhist monks developed the empty-hand system known as *te* ("hand"), importing new techniques from China. Eventually the new art was translated as *t'ang* ("China hand"), but was familiarly known as Okinawa-te ("Okinawa hand"). It was not until the 20th century that t'ang became known as karate-do ("empty hand"). The suffix *do* was added by Gichin Funakoshi's son Yoshitaka Funakoshi, in friendly opposition to his father's Okinawa-te style. Practice and demonstrations until that time had been extremely violent. Punches were not pulled and full contact was an integral part of the Okinawa-te style. Yoshitaka Funakoshi transformed the techniques of Okinawa-te into a gentler system, seeking not to deliver blows fully, but to "focus" strikes at skin level. The *do* suffix expressed the move away from the "aim of the warrior" and towards physical and spiritual development.

Gichin Funakoshi

Gichin Funakoshi (1868-1957) was a student of the Chinese classics and of the martial arts, and is credited with introducing karate to mainland Japan in the early part of the 20th century. Prior to this, in 1905, the occupying Japanese had authorized the inclusion of karate in the Okinawan physical education programme for middle school students. They appreciated the discipline inherent in karate and soon it became an integral part of the school educational system.

In 1917, at the request of the Japanese Ministry for Education, Funakoshi travelled from Okinawa to Kyoto in Japan and gave the first display of t'ang. In 1921, Funakoshi demonstrated his system for the Crown Prince of Japan at Shuri Castle. So impressive was this that Funakoshi was asked to appear at the first national athletic exhibition in Tokyo. Jiguro Kano, the founder of judo, among others, persuaded Funakoshi to stay on mainland Japan. In 1924, Funakoshi began teaching in several schools and *dojo* and founded the first University Karate Club at Keio University. Other styles started to develop, including kyokushinkai, shukukai and wado ryu. By 1936, karate had started to spread and the first purpose-built karate *dojo* was built, called shotokan (the "hall of shoto" – a pen name of

Funakoshi). The same year he published his second book, *Karate do Kyokan*.

In 1955 the first *dojo* of the Japan Karate Association was opened. Two years later in Tokyo, on 26 April, 1957, Funakoshi died. By this time, karate was well established, and today it is enjoyed throughout the world.

Styles

There are numerous styles of karate practised, and its influence even spreads into many other martial arts, so a book such as this cannot explore them all. This chapter will focus on the forms of wado ryu and shotokan. Hopefully, the information in this chapter will provide you with an insight into the world of karate, and allow you to decide if the discipline is for you.

It is also important to realize that the various styles of karate are the results of the personal ideas of many

Two senior karate sensei here illustrate attack and defence. Master Enoeda defends against Steve Arniel.

A senior student of Gichin Funakoshi – Hironori Ohtsuka – later devised his own "style" of karate: wado ryu.

Young children showing dedication to the art of karate.

individuals about how each basic technique should be carried out or applied. The different techniques within the styles of karate also dictate whether strength, speed, or hand or leg techniques are emphasized.

Karate as a sport

Karate has always been a self-defence system and a form of physical exercise. The competitive and sporting elements have a further part to play in the individual's enjoyment of this activity. It is because of the possibility of participation in competition that many people take up this art.

Competition comes in different forms, in which varying degrees of contact are allowed. In this book, we are concerned with traditional karate competition – sometimes termed sport karate. Certain dangerous techniques are omitted and strict rules are applied, making karate both safe and enjoyable for the competitor. One of the main purposes of karate competition is to show your skill at controlling the permitted techniques in a one-to-one combat situation. The individuals are allowed to move freely in a given area, which is controlled by a referee and a judge, or judges. *Kumite* is the word used to describe this type of competition.

Another form of competition that is also featured here is *kata*. *Kata* is a series of karate techniques performed alone against imaginary opponents. A *kata* competition resembles gymnastics or figure skating, in which points are awarded for correct technique and good balance, timing, rhythm, attitude and other attributes.

Competition is not the only reason for engaging in this art. It is possible to learn karate without participating in competitions – but for some people, competition provides stimulation and motivation for training. The sense of achievement that comes from just taking part, whether in *kata* or *kumite*, can be carried over into everyday life.

BENEFITS OF KARATE

The benefits derived from learning one of the forms of karate extend into many aspects of your everyday life. These include:

• Fitness, flexibility and mobility
• Well-being (through the balance of mind and body)
• Concentration and self-control
• Confidence
• Teamwork
• Honesty and integrity
• Stress reduction
• Sociability and courtesy

WADO RYU

history *and* philosophy

Hironori Ohtsuka (1892-1982) was the founder of the wado ryu system of karate. He commenced training in shindo yoshin ryu jujitsu at the age of six, and at the age of 30 he began training under the supervision of Gichin Funakoshi (the founder of karate-do) before founding the wado ryu system in 1939. Wado ryu is one of the four main Japanese styles of karate that are taught around the world. In 1939, Ohtsuka organized the All Japan Karate Do Federation Wado Ki and the Worldwide Headquarters for the Wado Ryu System. In 1967 he was the first *karateka* to be awarded the 5th order of merit of the sacred treasure of the Emperor of Japan as an acknowledgement of his achievements.

Following his death in 1982, Hironori Ohtsuka's son, Jiro, became the chief instructor of the wado ryu system. Today, there are a number of senior, well-respected representatives of wado ryu in Japan, who are also leaders of their own federations or associations.

Characteristics of wado ryu karate

To practitioners of wado ryu, the main philosophy is to better their attitude both within and outside the art. This is

Exhibition for the Crown Prince of Japan in 1921 at Shuri Castle.

Karate contains a number of airborne techniques.

The dove symbolizes a gentle or innocent person, as a means of advocating negotiation rather than violence.

one of the main aims of *budo* (martial art), which emphasizes the development of respect, discipline and understanding in a mental as well as physical capacity. This aim affects our attitude towards ourselves and others in our home life, work and social activities. To show aggression outwardly, even during training sessions, is greatly discouraged. The name wado ryu, approximately translated, means "the peaceful way".

Another characteristic of wado ryu is that unnecessarily large movements are kept to a minimum. Importance is placed on the speed and efficiency of movement with which each technique is performed, rather than the strength or physical effort outwardly shown. Exponents of wado ryu place great emphasis on the coordination of body movement with each particular technique. This principle is found in many other martial arts, such as ju-jitsu, aikido and kendo. This coordination is stressed at all stages of learning, from the execution of basic techniques to the application of advanced, free-fighting combinations.

Close quarter control is the underlying essence of karate.

BENEFITS OF WADO RYU

There are numerous benefits derived from learning wado ryu, which will extend into many aspects of everyday life. These include:

- Fitness
- Strength
- Confidence
- Self-discipline
- Self-control
- Sense of well-being

- Team work
- Concentration
- Integrity
- Sociability
- Courtesy

clothing *and* equipment

Karate practitioners wear a light, medium or heavy weight white cotton suit. The club badge or a combination is usually worn on the left side of the jacket. The white trousers have a drawstring waist and it is important to ensure you have the right size for comfort, practicality and safety. Protective equipment is used in karate by both men and women, especially in sparring (controlled fighting practice) and competition. Practitioners must be clean and tidy at all times, as a sign of respect to the art, teacher and fellow practitioner.

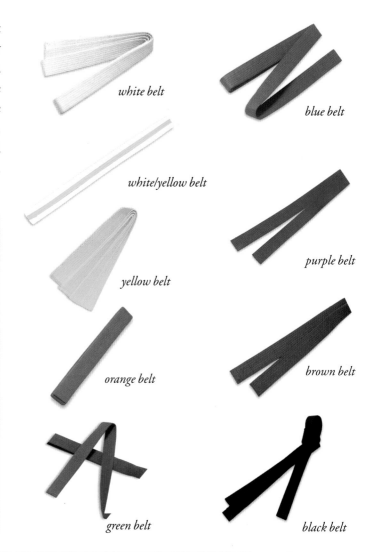

white belt

blue belt

white/yellow belt

yellow belt

purple belt

orange belt

brown belt

green belt

black belt

BELT GRADINGS

Beginners	White
10th-*kyu*	White
9th-*kyu*	White with yellow stripe
8th-*kyu*	Yellow
7th-*kyu*	Orange
6th-*kyu*	Green
5th-*kyu*	Blue
4th-*kyu*	Purple
3rd-*kyu*	Brown
2nd-*kyu*	Brown
1st-*kyu*	Brown
1st-*dan* and upwards	Black

PROTECTIVE EQUIPMENT
Extra protection in the form of groin protection (athletic cup) for men and breast protection for women are recommended for use at all times.

groin protection (athletic cup)

Bust protector

karate top

karate trousers

A smartly dressed karate instructor.

Etiquette

Training begins and ends with rituals of courtesy. These are an essential part of training and enable individuals to work safely and effectively together. Any distractions in a class could result in injury, and helping others to develop their abilities is an intrinsic part of being a good *karateka* (karate practitioner or student).

PRE-TRAINING DISCIPLINE

The instructor is always addressed by students as *sensei* (teacher or instructor). It is not quite accurate to translate *sensei* in this way, but for the sake of simplicity the word "teacher" will be used. It actually means "he who has gone before", indicating that whatever you are about to do or perform, your teacher will have done before, and understands its relevance.

There is nothing to distinguish one student (*karateka*) from another, other than the belt that is worn (*obi*), which is an acknowledgement of that person's experience. All *karateka* are equal as people, as indicated by a plain white cotton suit (*karate gi*). Juniors, seniors and masters alike must remove their footwear by the doorway and pause to bow (*rei*) before entering the training hall (*dojo*).

HELPFUL HINTS

- Training must be systematic, progressive and hard – technically as well as physically.
- Warm up before each training session and cool down afterwards.
- Constantly check and adjust the actions of individual techniques.
- Check the coordination of your movements for each technique.
- Practise all techniques using both sides of your body equally.
- Always be attentive to your opponent/ partner (*zanshin*).
- If available, use a mirror to monitor your movements during training.
- If available, use punch bags or pads as aids for correcting specific actions.

❶ △ Stand upright and relaxed, hands in front of your thighs and with your fingers together and straight, thumbs tucked in. Place your heels together with your feet angled outwards, forming a V shape.

❷ △ Perform a bow (*rei*) by lowering the top part of your body by no more than 45 degrees. Keep your back straight and bend from the hips. Keep your eyes looking forwards. Bring your body back to the upright position.

❸ △ Turn slightly to the left and lower your body into a squatting position. Place your hands on top of your knees, which should naturally splay apart. Keep looking forwards while you maintain your balance.

❹ △ Complete the kneeling position by first placing your right knee, then your left knee, on the floor. Check that the distance between your knees is approximately one fist-width. Your feet must not be crossed while in this kneeling position and the tops of your insteps should be flat on the floor.

5 ◁ To perform the bow (*rei*) bring both hands around your knees and place them on the floor in front of your body. Your forefingers and thumbs should be touching in the shape of a V. Lower your upper body to perform the bow, stopping when your face is, depending on your size, about 10 in (25 cm) from the floor – it is not correct for your head to touch your hands. The object is to try to maintain a level body posture with your head and back in a straight line.

THE BOW
The bow is usually performed two or three times before practice begins. The order of the bows is fixed: the first bow is to *Shomen* (the Founder); the second is to the teacher (who is usually positioned towards the east); and the third bow is to each other.

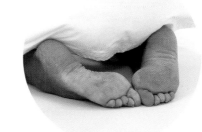

◁ Seen from the rear, your big toes are touching and your insteps are flat to the floor.

6 △ Straighten your back and sit back in the kneeling position, in preparation to stand.

7 △ Start to return to the standing position by stepping forward with your left foot. Note the position of the rear right foot.

8 △ Once you are on your feet and standing in the original start position, perform a final bow.

MEDITATION

This position demonstrates the meditation (*mokuso*) position, which you use to clear your mind and prepare yourself for the practice to come. Keep your back straight and your shoulders relaxed.

There are two possible hand positions during meditation. The first is to place your hands in an open position on top of your knees. The more common hand position, however, is the one demonstrated here. Turn your palms upwards into a cupped position with the tips of the thumbs touching. Close your eyes and try to clear your mind of any concerns, worries or anxieties. Aim for a feeling of calmness and tranquillity. It is good to concentrate on your breathing to help empty your mind of any thoughts that could be a distraction. Keep your breathing slow, deep and controlled by inhaling through your nose and breathing out through your mouth.

In a normal practice session, hold this position for a minimum of 60 seconds. You may wish to build up this exercise so that you can hold the position for longer periods as part of your relaxation routine. If you are not used to sitting like this, build the exercise up gradually. Never hold a position if you feel pain. There is a certain amount of discomfort in stretching or learning new exercises, so always take your time.

Exercise | Warm-up

The following depict some of the exercises which are incorporated in the warm-up and cooling-down sessions. To reduce the risk of injuries, sound advice should be sought prior to starting any fitness or exercise programme. Usually the instruction will determine the length of time and number of repetitions each exercise requires. All the following are held for 3–10 seconds.

WARM-UP 1 – *This series of movements is a very gentle exercise designed to loosen up the neck and so minimize the risk of any injury during the practice session. It helps to stretch the muscles at the back of your neck as well as helping to relieve tension.*

❶△ Stand in a relaxed position with your head upright.

❷△ Carefully lower your chin downwards towards your chest. Keep relaxed and gently push down as if nodding to say "yes". Hold for 6–10 seconds and then return your head to the upright position.

❸△ Continue the exercise with a side-neck stretch. Keep your head lowered and slowly move it towards your left shoulder.

❹▷ Keeping your head facing forward, slowly lower your head towards the top of your left shoulder to stretch the muscles in the right side of the neck for 3–4 seconds. Repeat this exercise, lowering your head towards the right shoulder to stretch the left neck muscles.

❺△ With the head in the upright position, turn your head so that you are looking over your right shoulder for 3 or 4 seconds. Repeat the exercise towards your left shoulder.

WARM-UP 2 – *The purpose of this series of exercises is to loosen and warm the body. This helps to avoid pulled muscles or torn ligaments during practice.*

❶ △ Keeping your arms bent from the elbows, rotate your arms in a full circular motion approximately 5–6 times, first clockwise, then anticlockwise (counterclockwise). This helps to stretch your shoulder muscles. Repeat 3–4 times in each direction.

❷ △ Stand in a relaxed position, feet apart. Push your left hand up and back five or six times. Reverse arm positions and repeat. This stretches your chest and shoulder muscles. Push back and release 2–4 times.

❸ △ Use a twisting motion to the right, bringing your arms in a circular action across your body and towards the rear. Repeat the exercise by turning towards the rear again. Hold for a few seconds then repeat the exercise to the left side.

❹ △ To stretch the sides of your body, stand in a relaxed position with your hands on your hips and feet apart. Lean slowly as far as possible to your right and extend your left arm as far as possible over your head. Hold for 3–10 seconds. Repeat the exercise to the opposite side by stretching your right arm towards your left side. Repeat this 2 or 3 times.

❺ △ Go into a squatting position and tuck your bottom in. Extend both arms forwards as far as possible at shoulder height. Hold this position for 3–10 seconds. This is excellent for stretching your lower back.

❻ △ With your legs fairly wide apart, slowly bend your right knee to lower your body towards that side. Hold at your lowest point for 3–10 seconds to stretch your inner thighs. Repeat this exercise to the other side and alternate 2 or 3 times.

❼ △ From an upright position, turn your body to the right. Come up on to the ball of your left foot and lower your body by bending your right knee. Hold the position at its lowest point for 3–10 seconds. Repeat to the left and alternate 2 or 3 times. This stretches your inner and upper thighs.

❽ ◁ From an upright position, move your right foot slightly in front of your left, keeping your back as flat as possible. Slowly lower your body, as if bowing from the waist, into a forwards position with your arms hanging forwards. Hold at your lowest point for 3–10 seconds, or longer if comfortable. Bend both knees before returning to the upright position. Repeat, starting with the left foot forward, and alternate 2 or 3 times.

❾ ▷ From a squatting position, move forwards on to your hands with your body raised – like a sprinter's start position in the blocks. Slowly press one heel down and backwards towards the floor. Hold for 3–10 seconds. Repeat the exercise with your other foot flat to the floor and alternate 4 or 5 times. This stretches your calf muscles.

Technique | *Kata – Pinan nidan*

The *kata – pinan nidan –* shown below is one of the first introduced to low grade students in most karate styles, with variation of technique depending on the particular style. *Kata* are a compilation of individual techniques put into various sequences, in which a practitioner encounters one or more imaginary opponent(s).

❶ ◁ Take a few moments to focus your concentration on your imaginary opponent(s). Stand with your shoulders relaxed and make sure that your hands are open and lightly touching your thighs. *Note: a* kata *is designed to enable the practitioner to respond, defend and counter from a number of different angles and attackers. Emphasis is placed on good posture, coordination, timing and understanding basic technique and its application.*

❷ ▷ Perform the bow (*rei*). Bow from the waist, but avoid bending too far forward. Keep your eyes alert and looking ahead.

◁ This is a side angle view of the bow.

❸ ▷ To remain in a central position, and prepare for the natural standing position, *shizentai*, first move your left leg away from your right, followed by moving your right leg slightly away from your left leg. You should then be in a balanced position, with your feet shoulder-width apart, still splayed at approximately 20 degrees.

❹ △ Move your left leg towards the left, dropping your body weight by bending your knees. At the same time take your left arm in a circular motion (as the arrow suggests) to your left side to perform the defence (*tetsui otoshi uke*). The bottom of the left fist is used to strike while the right fist is pulled back to your side. Keep your elbows tucked in.

❺ △ Step through with your right leg, striking at the aggressor's solar plexus (*junzuki chudan*) with the right fist. For the next move, you will step to the rear, turning your body 180 degrees, following the direction of the arrows.

❻ △ When you turn, perform a lower defence action (*gedan barai*) in a clockwise direction. This technique will stop a kick or punch aimed at your lower body.

❼ △ Pull the right front leg backwards as you perform the hammer fist (*tetsui otoshi uke*) downward circular defence. The fist depicts a "hammer", hence the term, and can be used as both a defence and strike to an opponent.

8 ◁ Step through with your left leg and strike with your left fist to the opponent's solar plexus. Prepare to turn to the left, as the arrow shows, for the next move.

9 ▷ Turn and perform the lower sweeping defence (*gedan barai*). Keep your body upright, shoulders relaxed, and legs well braced. The key points of this stance are: feet a shoulder-width apart, back straight, eyes forward, back leg straight and a good bend on the front leg with your knee in line with your toes.

10 △ Step forwards with your right foot and perform an upper rising defence with your right arm to protect your head. Take care not to obscure your own vision by, for example, allowing your arm to cover your eyes. Bring your right arm up across your body, ensuring you completely cover the torso as you raise your arm, as if aiming for your left shoulder. Push your arm upwards and slightly backwards to ensure your defence fully covers your head.

11 △ Step through with your left foot and perform the same upper rising defence with your left arm. It is important to have a 45-degree bend on the forearm so that any attack is deflected, not met square-on. In this way, a blow making contact with the arm should slide downwards and away from you. If the forearm is horizontal, too much force will be directed on to one point and the result could be severe bruising, a fracture or a break.

12 ▷ Step through for a third time, performing the same upper rising defence with your right arm and using *kiai*. This is where you exhale with a short, sharp sound to emphasize your focus. The shout, or scream as it is sometimes called, can cause fear or distract your opponent. In the next move, your left leg will follow the direction of the arrow to the left, to initiate a turn.

13 △ Leading with your left leg, turn anticlockwise (counterclockwise) and utilize the lower sweeping defence.

14 △ Step through, right leg forward, and punch at your opponent's solar plexus with your right fist (*junzuki chudan*).

15 △ Move across to the right side, again performing the lower sweeping defence.

16 △ Step through with your left leg and punch with your left fist at your opponent's solar plexus (*junzuki chudan*).

17 △ Move 45 degrees in an anticlockwise (counterclockwise) direction and perform the lower sweeping defence.

18 △ Step through with your right leg and punch with your right fist to the solar plexus (*junzuki chudan*).

19 △ Step through again for a second *junzuki chudan* strike with your left leg and left fist forward.

20 △ Step through for a third time, with your right foot and right fist forward, and perform the *junzuki chudan* strike, this time using your shout (*kiai*).

21 △ Bring your left leg behind and across the rear of your body, turning in an anticlockwise (counterclockwise) direction into a cat stance, *neko ashi dachi*. About 70 per cent of your weight should be on your right leg. You are now in a position ready to defend and counter.

22 △ As you move through from one stance to another, try to maintain the same height i.e. do not push the body upwards or lower the body as you move forwards to each stance. By doing this, you make it more difficult for the aggressor to detect your intended movements.

23 △ Step through with your right leg, still maintaining the same body height, and keep your left arm extended.

24 ◁ Strike at your imaginary opponent with your open right hand, aiming at the lower abdomen (*yoko nukite*).

25 ▷ Take your right leg through 90 degrees into the cat stance (*neko ashi dachi*), with your right hand, palm uppermost, above the left, in preparation to strike. Reach forwards with your right leg in preparation for the next move.

26 ◁ Twist your body into a low stance (*shiko ashi dachi*) to perform the lower open-hand strike with your right hand. In the next move, you will step through with your left leg, in the direction of the arrow.

27 ◁ Step through with your left leg in preparation for the final strike.

28 ◁ Twist your body and strike, as previously, with your open left hand to the lower body (*yoko nukite*). In the next move, your left leg will move backwards in the direction of the arrow.

29 △ Now bring your left leg back to resume the upright standing position (*shizentai*).

30 △ Bring the left foot in, followed by the right, with the back of your heels together and feet splayed.

31 △ Bow again from the waist to complete the *kata* sequence. Maintain a calm and respectful manner, and keep alert until you have walked away from the practice area.

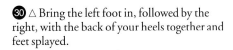

Technique | Two-person exercises – *Kumite*

Developing techniques in wado ryu is achieved through practising with a partner. The highest respect and discipline must always be maintained to preserve the values of the art and also to prevent injury. The following demonstrates the initial etiquette in preparation for the two-person practice (*kumite*) and some basic defence and striking actions.

❶ △ Stand opposite your partner in the ready position approximately one metre's distance (minimum arm and a half distance).

❷ △ Perform the etiquette bow (*rei*), keeping your eyes on your partner all the time.

❸ △ Move into a stance known as the *hidari shizentai* position, ready to perform the techniques. In this position, the left foot is slightly forward in preparation to defend or attack.

❹ △ You are grabbed at the front by your partner's left hand.

❺ △ Perform a circular action with your left arm to enable the grip to be broken, stepping through with your left leg in preparation for the arm lock.

❻ △ Once you have completed the circular movement, your opponent's grip will be broken and your partner will be in a vulnerable position.

❼ ◁ Move through with your right leg and apply pressure to his left arm by maintaining the arm lock and strong upright posture.

❽ ▷ Step through with your right leg and go into a deep (low) stance. Your partner's arm is now fully trapped by the application of pressure on his upper arm from your right elbow. From this position you can maintain the resraint or apply another technique that is applicable.

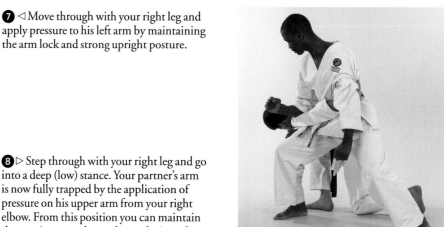

Technique | Blocking

Blocking is the term used to describe the defence method of arresting an attack, whether it be from an arm or leg strike. Various parts of the body, such as the forearm, palm heel and elbow, are used in a variety of ways to defend against an on-coming attack. This is complemented by the correct body movement for the nature of the attack.

1 △ Step to the side and deflect your partner's kick by using a left lower forearm defence. The hand is made into a fist and a short circular action is used to deflect the kick. Note the right hand guard position.

2 △ Pull your deflecting left arm around in a circular motion, bringing it down across your partner's neck and face. This action will push your partner backwards and off balance.

3 ◁ A possible follow-on from this technique is to pull around behind your partner and apply a neck lock.

◁ Here you can see a more detailed side view of the previous neck lock.

Technique | Defence

There are a variety of very effective defensive moves in wado ryu which can be applied in a self-defence situation. The following is one such technique which demonstrates a combination of blocks and strikes, utilizing both hands and feet for different parts of the body.

❶ △ Your partner moves through with his right leg and right fist, aiming a punch at your face.

❷ ◁ Defend by stepping back and angling yourself slightly to the right. Use your left hand to deflect the blow downwards and, simultaneously, counter-strike with the palm of your right hand, aiming for the side of his jaw (mandible) – or deliver a front strike to his chin. Timing is important and the area to aim at depends on which is more accessible.

△ This angle of the action in step 2 shows how you deliver the palm blow.

❸ ▷ Pivot on your left leg and lift your right knee in preparation to strike with the top part of your foot to your partner's groin area.

△ In this close-up of step 2, you can see that the strike has been focused on the inner top part of the thigh. This is essential when practising to avoid injuring your partner. It is also advisable to wear groin protection when practising this type of technique.

Technique | *Taisabaki*

The following is a sample of three of the many *taisabaki* (evasive) techniques practised in wado ryu. The main principles behind these techniques consist of evasive manoeuvres to avoid contact if possible. *Taisabaki* practice increases the ability of the practitioner to move quickly in a variety of direction and be at an advantage to counter-strike.

❶ ◁ As your partner moves in towards you with his left leg forward and right fist aimed towards your head, you should lean backwards to avoid contact.

❷ ◁ As your partner steps through with *mai te zuki* (front punch delivered with the same arm and leg forward, or, right punch, right leg), drop and twist towards the right and take your left shoulder down towards the floor.

❸ ▷ A defence against a *maigeri* (front kick) is achieved by twisting and side-stepping to avoid the kick.

SHOTOKAN

松濤館

history *and* philosophy

Shotokan karate is both a young and an ancient martial art. It is ancient because its roots are deeply entrenched in the past, and young because, as it is expressed today, it is an art that is less than a hundred years old. Shotokan is characterized by its long, low stances, its powerful techniques and its dynamic forms.

The "founder" of shotokan, Gichin Funakoshi, was an Okinawan. He trained in the oldest of the Okinawan *te* ("hand") systems as a young man and in the early 20th century brought what he had learned in the island of Okinawa to mainland Japan, where he demonstrated his art before the Emperor. He originally intended to return to Okinawa but was persuaded to remain and continue teaching in Japan. Funakoshi's pen name was Shoto (which means "waving pines"), and *kan* means "hall", so shotokan karate can be translated to mean, "Shoto's hall of the way of the empty hand".

While Funakoshi was the orignator of shotokan, it was really his son, Yoshitaka Funakoshi, who developed it into the form we know today. It rapidly grew in popularity, supported, encouraged and regulated by the powerful Japan Karate Association, and before long was to be found all over the world.

Shotokan has produced some of the world's greatest karate exponents, including Hirokazu Kanazawa. It is believed by many *karateka* (karate practitioners) that Hirokazu has come closest to possessing the most perfect technique. He studied karate at Takushoku University and won all the Japan Championships in 1962, with a broken hand after his mother had persuaded him to fight. Shotokan continues to be practised by thousands of people, adults and children, throughout the world.

Triads

Shotokan karate is built on what are known as "triads", which are both real organizations and metaphors for some-

Early days of shotokan karate in a dojo *in Tokyo. Notice the traditional* tatami *mat flooring.*

thing much deeper within the human psyche. There exists the physical triad of *kihon* (basics), *kumite* (sparring) and *kata* (forms), which require dedicated training and the constant perfecting of technique. This is followed by the moral triad of justice, mercy and compassion and finally by the ethical triad of duty, honour and loyalty.

If you put all of the nine triad principles together (nine symbolizes perfection) you achieve the whole, rounded person. When these principles are practised in a martial art, they illustrate one of the fundamental concepts of shotokan karate, as advocated by the founder, Gichin Funakoshi. His aim was to focus on the development of the human character as a whole being, rather than on winning and losing.

Quite apart from the normal reasons why somebody would take up a martial art, such as self-defence, there are other reasons that, while they may not be clear at the time, emerge during the course of training. Shotokan not only provides the means to defend yourself against an aggressor, it also gives you a sense of self-confidence. Self-confidence stimulates a sense of well-being and a greater sense of awareness when in difficult situations. It also heightens your consciousness of the environment and the very nature of unjust aggression. In this context, the *karateka* (students of karate) can make a mature and reasoned judgement as to what response, if any, to make – provided, of course, that the response conforms to the rules laid down by law, governing the use of reasonable force.

In this sense, shotokan (and the pursuit of excellence) brings with it grave responsibilities that must be exercised with compassion and mercy. The physical development and improvement of technique and ability is useless without this other dimension. Ultimately, karate exists to perfect the individual, to produce men and women who are just,

Taiji Kase, a senior member of the shotokan fraternity, illustrates the Chinese influence upon modern-day karate.

compassionate and honourable members of society, people who recognize injustice and, through their own behaviour, challenge it.

While shotokan is a wonderful form of relaxation or sport for many people, for those who practise it seriously it has a much wider and deeper significance. But this deeper realization can come only after years of dedicated practice. While this is a dimension of the art that emerges only slowly, karate can still be enjoyed at all levels by hundreds of thousands of people throughout the world.

Harada Sensei, a direct student of Gichin Funakoshi, defends against a double-wrist grab.

BENEFITS OF SHOTOKAN

The benefits derived from learning shotokan extend into many aspects of your everyday life. These include:

- Fitness, flexibility and mobility
- Well-being (through the balance of mind and body)
- Concentration and self-control
- Confidence and assertiveness
- Teamwork
- Honesty, integrity and humility
- Appreciation of justice and fair play
- Stress reduction
- Sociability and courtesy

clothing *and* equipment

Shotokan practitioners wear a white cotton top and drawstring trousers. Most schools follow the belt grading system below, with beginners usually wearing a white or blue belt.

At 3rd-*dan* a *karateka* may be addressed as "*sensei*". At 4th-*dan* it is assumed that the *karateka* is well acquainted with the style and has a deep knowledge of the technical syllabus. A 5th-*dan* can be awarded after the writing of a technical thesis on karate. All *dan* grade awards after this are for progress within shotokan, with emphasis on style, devotion, dedication and commitment to the art. With the award of 6th-*dan* can come the title "*shihan*" which freely translated means "master" or literally "a teacher of teachers". At this stage the *karateka* is regarded as a master of his/her style and is given the right to wear the red and white belt or may continue to wear the black belt. Although it may take 30 years of hard, disciplined training and study to achieve 6th-*dan*, this may only be the beginning of the pursuit of excellence.

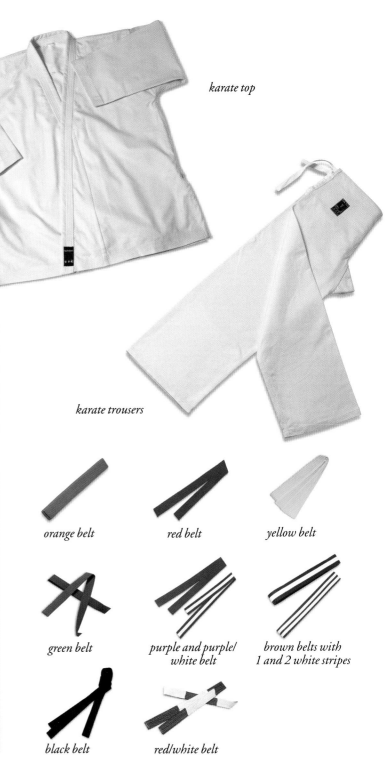

karate top

karate trousers

orange belt

red belt

yellow belt

green belt

purple and purple/ white belt

brown belts with 1 and 2 white stripes

black belt

red/white belt

BELT GRADINGS

9th-*kyu*	Orange
8th-*kyu*	Red
7th-*kyu*	Yellow
6th-*kyu*	Green
5th-*kyu*	Purple
4th-*kyu*	Purple with white stripe
3rd-*kyu*	Brown
2nd-*kyu*	Brown with one white stripe
1st-*kyu*	Brown with two white stripes
1st–5th-*dan*	Black
5th-*dan* upwards	Black or red and white

Etiquette

In shotokan karate there are three types of bow (*rei*) used in different circumstances – namely: *shomen ni rei*, performed as a sign of respect to the training area; *otagani rei*, performed to the great masters of the past and present; and *shihan rei*, which is used by both teachers and students.

OTAGANI REI – *Bow performed to the great masters of the past and present.*

1 △ Stand in a natural position (*hachichi dachi*), with your feet splayed slightly outwards and with your hands hanging relaxed at the sides of your body. Keep looking forwards.

2 △ Move your right leg in towards your left so that your heels are touching.

3 △ Turn your left shoulder forwards.

4 △ Lower your body towards the floor, placing your left knee on the floor and make sure that you keep looking forwards.

5 △ Place your right knee on the floor, aligning it with your left, and place your hands on top of your thighs.

6 △ Leaning slightly forwards from the kneeling position (*seiza*), place your left hand in front of your body.

7 △ Follow through with your right hand so that your forefingers and thumbs make a triangular shape. Make sure that you keep looking forwards.

8 △ Bend forwards from the waist, keeping your fingers in the same position and your gaze forwards. Reverse the process back into kneeling and stand.

Exercise | Warm-up

In shotokan karate, the warm-up exercises are very similar to those in wado ryu karate, covered in the first section of this chapter. Those below are just a sample of the exercises performed prior to a training session. Make sure that you approach every exercise gently and with caution. Build up at your own pace to an acceptable and comfortable level.

WARM-UP 1 – *This exercise is designed to stretch your triceps, back and chest area.*

◁ Bring your left arm across the back of your head and place your right hand on your left elbow. Pull your elbow in a downwards motion towards your right side. Repeat 2 to 3 times each side.

▷ This is a rear view of the position when the exercise is performed on the other side. It shows the correct arm and hand positions, with your right hand on the left shoulder blade and your left hand gripping your right elbow.

WARM-UP 2 – *The following movement exercises the fingers and assists in making the wrists more supple.*

❶ △ Push your hand downwards and outwards, keeping your fingers open and splayed.

❷ △ Push your fingers well back, with your palm facing upwards, using a downwards rocking motion. Hold this position for several seconds and perform the same exercise on the opposite side. Repeat the whole exercise once more.

WARM-UP 3 – *This exercise is beneficial for your back, hips and thighs promoting suppleness and flexibility.*

▷ Sit on the floor and cross your right leg over your left, keeping your right knee bent. Look to the rear so that you stretch the upper part of your body as well as the lower back, hip and upper thighs. Make sure that your right hand is placed well behind you so that you feel securely balanced. Place your left arm across the outside of your right knee and twist your body backwards. Hold this position for approximately 20 seconds, then reverse leg and hand positions and repeat 2 or 3 times each side.

WARM-UP 4 – *This exercise stretches your inner thighs and leg muscles and promotes good body balance.*

WARM-UP 5 – *This exercise will stretch the back of your thighs and calf muscles.*

△ Place your right leg to the side to adopt a wide stance. Then carefully lower your body so that your left knee is well bent and your right leg is straight, toes facing forwards. Keep your hands stretched out in front of you, palms facing forwards, and your right hand gripping your left. If you have not performed this, or a similar exercise before, it may take a lot of practice to maintain your balance while stretching. Hold this position for approximately 20 seconds, then reverse leg positions and repeat 2 or 3 times for each side.

△ Place your left foot in front of your right, with your heel down and toes facing up. Place both hands on your left thigh, pushing your hips back and leaning forwards with the top part of your body. Hold for several seconds and reverse the leg position. Repeat 2 to 3 times.

Technique | Basics

Learning a series of basic techniques has always been very important to all martial art traditions. In this way, you build a good foundation on which all moves can be correctly and safely executed. Some of these moves will be common to two or more different martial arts, while others may be unique.

ZENKUTSU DACHI – Shotokan, in particular, is well known for its use of a very low stance called zenkutsu dachi, or front stance. This is used in the majority of the basic moves.

△ From the natural position, with your feet shoulder-width apart, step forwards into a low stance with your left leg. Keep your back leg straight with the heel flat on the floor. Make sure the knee of your leading leg is bent to an angle of approximately 90 degrees.

JUDACHI – This stance is a shorter version of the front stance and is more suitable for close-quarter combat, competition and basic self-defence moves.

◁ Note that your legs should not be positioned as low as in the classic front stance. Keep both hands in a protective position in front of your body. Practise this stance, moving forwards and backwards with both your right and left legs.

KOKUTSU DACHI – An effective defensive move.

△ Step forwards with your left leg, distributing your body weight so that about 70 per cent is on the rear leg. Hold your hands in a protective open hand (fingers straight) position, with the right hand covering the solar plexus and the left hand in the guard position ready to defend or strike. Practise on both sides.

KIBA DACHI – This position is known as the horse stance.

△ Move your right leg to the side into a low posture similar to that of riding a horse. The knees must be bent well forwards, with heels parallel to each other and feet facing forwards. Keep your back straight and your hands in a closed hand (fist) guard position. Practise this stance, moving forwards and backwards alternating between your left and right leg.

NEKO ASHI DACHI – *The feeling of feline lightness and poise gives this position its name of "cat stance".*

◁ Move forwards with your left leg, ensuring that about 90 per cent of your weight is on the back leg. Practise this stance, moving forwards and backwards with both your right and left legs. Ensure that your knees are well bent and your right hand is placed on your right hip ready to execute a technique, while your left hand is in the lower guard position.

SANSHIN DACHI – *The hand and foot positions give the figure a pinched-looking middle, accounting for its name of "hour-glass stance".*

◁ With your feet about a shoulder-width apart and your right foot slightly in front, turn your feet inwards and slightly bend your knees. Keep your back upright, chin straight and eyes looking forwards. The hands are in the ready position to strike, with the left hand at shoulder level and right hand on the waist. Use the palm heel to strike both the face and groin simultaneously. Repeat on the other side.

FUDA DACHI (SOCHIN) – *Because of the very low, strong body position, this is known as "the rooted stance".*

▷ Move forwards with your leading leg, ensuring that about 90 per cent of your weight is on the back leg. Practise this stance, moving forwards and backwards with both your right and left legs. This low posture is excellent for developing strong calves and thigh muscles. The clenched fists are positioned to protect the face and body prior to striking, if necessary.

GUARD POSITION

It is very important to protect your body when being confronted and/or practising. The stance you adopt will dictate the most appropriate hand guard position. This can vary from having both hands in front of the torso, with one hand just above the other, to having one hand in front of the face (but not obscuring vision) and the other in the lower body region. This strategic position ensures the body is effectively covered and ready either to defend or to strike.

Technique | Defence and blocking

Shotokan embodies a variety of defence and blocking techniques. *Kata* (set forms where the practitioner defends and strikes an imaginary opponent) also differ in application and shotokan has, in addition, its own unique *kata*. The following are a sample of two of the basic blocking techniques used. They can be practised in isolation or with a partner.

SOTO UKE (BODY BLOCK) – *This is a defensive move against an attack to the chest (middle body) area.*

❶ ◁ Stand with feet together and bring your right arm in line with the back of your head. Simultaneously bring your left arm in front of your upper chest. As you start to move forwards with your right leg, into a low stance, bring your right fist through in a circular motion. At the same time, pull your left hand back on to your left hip.
Note: Imagine you have a piece of string attached to both hands, and as the left hand pulls back, so it brings the right arm into position.

❷ ◁ Keep looking towards your opponent and maintain a strong posture as you deliver this technique. Keep your left fist well back on your left hip and right arm in a bowed position. Aim to use the inside of your forearm, near the elbow, when delivering the block against the opponent's strike.

GEDAN BARAI (LOWER BODY BLOCK)

◁ From the natural position (*hachichi dachi*), make a fist with both hands and bring your left fist across your chest, in line with your right collar bone. Step forwards with your left foot into *zenkutsu dachi* stance. At the same time, bring the left arm across your body in a downwards motion to finish with the left fist approximately 4–5 inches (10–13 cm) above the left knee. This blocking action is very effective against lower body strikes, especially kicking techniques.

Technique | Kicking

Shotokan embodies a selection of strong kicking techniques to the front, side and rear of the body. Kicking techniques have two applications. The first is *keage* (shown here), which means to strike in a "snapping action", such as kicking with a fast retraction. The second variation is *kekome*, which emphasises thrusting and using the heel.

1 △ Move into the low horse stance (*kiba dachi*). Make sure that your hands are in the guard position.

2 △ Bring your left leg across your right, making sure that the knees are locked in a "scissor" position.

3 ▷ With your guard still in position, bring your right leg up to the side of your body and push outwards, striking towards one of your imaginary opponent's vulnerable areas, such as the face, solar plexus, floating rib or groin. This is known as *yoko geri*. Make sure that you twist your foot to the side so that the "knife edge" of the foot will be tense – this is the part that delivers the technique. To assist in this action, push your toes inwards and downwards while keeping your foot horizontal.

4 ◁ Bring your kicking foot back in a snapping action, in line with your left knee. It is important to bring your foot back before going down into a fighting posture, to avoid having your leg swept away from under you. It also allows you the freedom to choose where you wish to position your stance: forwards, side or back.

5 ▷ Go back down into the *kiba dachi* posture, still in fighting stance, keeping your eyes on your opponent.

Technique | *Soto uke* block

It is very important to practise basic techniques, such as this blocking/counter-attacking exercise, working from both right and left positions. If you are right-handed and have a weak left hand/foot, work twice as hard with the left side so that you can balance the strength of your skill. This applies to all techniques.

❶△ Bow to show respect to your partner. Remember the "respect but no trust" principle, which is why it is important to look at your opponent, not down towards the floor.

❷ △ Your partner steps back with his right foot, preparing to strike your solar plexus region. Note the low front posture (*zenkutsu dachi*).

❸ ◁ You step back with your right leg into the formal *zenkutsu dachi* stance and defend with the middle body block (*chudan soto uke*). This is a block from outside inwards. Apply this defence by starting with your left fist in line with your left ear and, using a circular motion, bring your arm forwards, around and across your body. Make sure you turn your forearm inwards so that it is the muscle part of the arm that makes contact with the incoming blow. At the same time, pull your left shoulder back so that your body turns to the side, thus becoming a smaller target.

4 ◁ Whether you block with your left or right arm dictates where you punch your opponent. In this case, when you have executed your block, use a downwards motion to push the attacking arm away. A circular action draws the opponent or partner off-centre and exposes his chest area in preparation for your counter-attack, a front-lunge punch (*oi-tsuki*).

5 ▽ Deliver a strike to your opponent's solar plexus region with your right fist. Remember to maintain a low, strong posture (*zenkutsu dachi*).

Technique | Elbow strike and wrist take-down

The following demonstrates a sequence of moves utilizing *soto uke* block, elbow strike (*empi*) and wrist locks (*kokuto*) to restrain the opponent. There are various sequences in shotokan where the basics are applied and developed incorporating more advanced techniques. It is important to utilize your strengths against the opponent's weaknesses.

❶◁ Step back and perform *soto uke* block to the right fist attack from your opponent.

❷▷Immediately follow through with an elbow *empi* strike to the hinge of your opponent's jaw.

❸▷ Bring your right hand back to your opponent's right wrist in preparation to apply a wrist turn and lock.

△ This close-up shows in detail the position of your hands and fingers on your opponent's hand.

4 ▽ Start to rotate your opponent's wrist by turning the hand outwards so that the palm is facing upwards. Next, ensure your thumbs are secure on the back of his hand, with your fingers firmly wrapped around his lower hand and wrist.

◁ This close-up shows in more detail the position of your hands and fingers on your opponent's hand.

5 △ Maintain the lock and keep the momentum going as you start to push the hand downwards, forcing your opponent to submit.

6 ▽ Continue to push downwards so that your partner will be restrained on the floor.

7 ▷ As your opponent reaches the floor, bring your left leg forwards and over his right arm. Aim to turn your body 180 degrees and apply pressure on his elbow joint as your body moves over his right arm.

8 ▷ The follow-on advanced technique is an arm lock. Bring your right leg over and across your opponent's arm and turn around so that you are facing in the opposite direction. Slowly lower your body so as to apply pressure on his elbow joint and form an arm lock. When practising with a partner always take care to apply this technique slowly and with caution.
Note: This is an advanced technique which requires qualified supervision.

AIKIDO

Aikido is an art that teaches one to harmonize completely with any attack, leading an aggressor to a point of imbalance, and then applying a neutralizing technique. Some practitioners believe that it is possible to study aikido as a spiritual discipline alone, whereby students learn to unite their spiritual energy with the universe to become "one with nature". It is equally possible to study aikido as a dynamic system of combat. For most individuals, however, the reality of aikido training falls between these two positions.

AIKIDO

history *and* philosophy

Aikido in its present form is a relatively recent innovation within the martial arts tradition, and was developed in Japan in the early 20th century by Morihei Ueshiba (1883-1969), who was introduced to the classical martial arts as a boy by his father, Yoroku. He is known to have studied some martial arts, such as various styles of ju-jitsu as well as kenjutsu and the art of the spear. In 1912 Morihei moved to Hokkaido, where a chance meeting with a man called Sokaku Takeda changed his life.

Takeda was a master of daito ryu-aiki ju-jutsu, a martial art that had originated in the 6th century AD and had been passed down through the military hierarchy and formalized by members of the Aizu clan, becoming known as the Oshikiuchi, or "striking arts". The young Ueshiba quickly became drawn to the fierce demeanour of this little man, and studied under Takeda until 1919. On returning to his native Tanabe on the death of his father, Morihei met Onisaburo Deguchi – the charismatic founder of an esoteric religion called Omoto-Kyo – and spent the next six years as his disciple, travelling throughout Asia.

In 1927, Morihei set up the Kobukan *dojo* in Tokyo and began teaching an amalgam of the martial traditions he had learned from Takeda, together with the spiritual beliefs he had gleaned from Deguchi. This new discipline he called Ueshiba aiko-budo. Morihei finally settled on the name of aikido. This word is a combination of three concepts: *ai*

meaning "harmony"; *ki* meaning "spirit"; and *do* meaning "way". In the spiritual sense, this means harmonizing your individual spirit, or *ki*, with the spirit of Nature itself. In the *dojo*, this means that you harmonize with an attack, lead it to a point of exhaustion and then neutralize it with a throw, joint lock, or an immobilization.

As with many other martial arts, aikido is seen not only as a system of self-defence, but also as a means of self-cultivation and improvement. Today there are various systems of aikido, but traditional aikido has no tournaments, competitions or contests. Physical strength is not a prerequisite, so age is no impediment. According to Morihei Ueshiba, the goal of aikido is not the defeat of others, but the defeat of the negative characteristics that inhabit one's own mind and inhibit its effective functioning.

What is aikido?

If you look at the classic Chinese *yin* and *yang* icon, you see a symbol explaining that all phenomena are governed by antagonistic, yet complementary opposites, forming the two halves of the whole. You will also observe that the two halves are not entirely opposite, however, since they have elements of each other within them – the black dot in the white half and white dot in the black half – and this esoteric symbolism is designed to suggest that all of life and nature is in a perpetual state of flux.

The antagonistic yet complementary opposites of the Chinese yin *and* yang *icon underly the philosophy behind aikido.*

If you are attacked by a force (*yang*) and you apply force yourself (*yang*), a collision of energies ensues which results in disharmony, and accordingly the strongest force wins. If, however, you meet that force with an absorbing movement (*yin*) and then exhaust it to the point of imbalance before applying a force of your own (the aikido way), you are, in effect, restoring harmony or redressing an imbalance. This is the basic logic and underlying philosophy of aikido.

Aikido is a discipline that seeks not to meet violence with violence, but instead looks towards harmonizing with and restraining an opponent. Aikido is, in many ways, unique among the martial arts, in that the majority of techniques are based on the aggressor making the first move. Therefore, aikido techniques are usually aimed at joint immobilization, and throws which utilize an opponent's energy, momentum and aggression. Many body movements have been taken from Japanese sword and spear fighting arts, and the use of the *bokken*, (a replica sword), and *jo* (a stick), is intended to develop the practitioner's understanding and skill.

Aikido teaches one-on-one and multiple-attack defence. It incorporates knife-taking, sword- and stick-taking, and even defence from a kneeling position. Differences in size, weight, strength or age are negated, as you learn to use your inner *ki* (flow of energy). Weapon training with a *bokken* and *jo* indicates the ancestry of the discipline as well as helping to improve your body movements. Most of these techniques are covered in this book.

It should be emphasized that aikido is a *budo* – literally a "martial way". You practise each technique with total commitment, as if your life depended on its success, for only in this way is it possible to bring about the true spirit of *budo*. This is not to say that training has to be hard or violent: it is possible to be physically soft and still generate the power to control a confrontational encounter.

Training

By training cooperatively with a partner, you can practise even potentially lethal techniques without risk, but professional supervision and safe practice are always required for students to avoid injury. Mutual respect and the careful consideration of what you are learning, together with its consequences, must always be your main concern. There are no shortcuts or easy paths to ability in aikido. Attaining proficiency is simply a matter of sustained and dedicated training, just as it is in many of the martial arts disciplines. Nobody becomes an expert in a few months.

While there are different styles of aikido – such as tomiki, or sport aikido, in which rubber knives are used and practitioners compete to score points – the founder, Morihei Ueshiba, was firmly opposed to competition in any form.

Styles of aikido

In reality, there are several major styles of aikido today. As Ueshiba was continually refining and modifying the art he had created, some of his students at various stages left to pursue their own ideals. Thus, Master Gozo Shioda created the yoshinkan style, characterized by short, sharp movements and powerful joint applications; Kenji Tomiki created sport aikido, as it is widely known, characterized by competitions in which rubber knives are used; Minoru Mochizuki successfully amalgamated aikido with other martial arts within the International Martial Arts Federation; and Koichi Tohei created shin-shin toitsu aikido, which concentrates on the *ki* aspect of aikido. All of these men trained with and listened to Ueshiba and yet each came away with a different idea of the discipline.

The grading system

The grading in aikido consists of *kyu* (student) grades, 6th to 1st, after which students become eligible for a 1st-*dan* (1st-

Demonstrating one of aikido's flowing movements and flexibility of practitioners.

Demonstrating the dynamics of aikido in action, showing gyaku *(reverse)* kotegaeshi *(outward wrist twist).*

degree black belt), and then 2nd-*dan*, 3rd-*dan* and so on. These gradings are based on a National grading syllabus and are spaced apart according to the dictate of the clubs' governing association.

There are no coloured belts in traditional aikido, except for children. This is in accordance with directives from the *hombu* (headquarters) in Japan. Because there are no weight or strength divisions, it is possible for men, women and children to train together, although certain techniques are eliminated from children's practice for safety reasons.

As a first step, students learn how to fall properly and how to absorb the effects of the various techniques, so that they can be performed with total commitment. Next is the freestanding solo body movements, where students learn about shifting weight, balance and similar aspects of the discipline. Finally, the techniques themselves are taught, and the degree of difficulty is dependent on each individual's own progress.

Benefits of aikido

People learn aikido for a variety of reasons: as a way of becoming physically fit, as self-defence, or to understand something of Japanese culture. It is up to each individual to decide upon which facet of the discipline to concentrate. In addition to the development of strength, stamina and suppleness, students learn to tap their internal powers to generate an energy that is far greater than muscular power alone, and to use it at will. Students may also find mental stimulation in knowing that they are practising movements dating back to Japan's feudal past.

Breathing techniques are learned to promote mind and body coordination. Students also come into contact with other Japanese practices, such as shiatsu (finger therapy), a form of total body massage, and iaido (Japanese sword drawing). Both of these disciplines are complementary to the study of aikido and are occasionally taught in tandem.

BENEFITS OF AIKIDO

Aikido offers many benefits to enhance health and well-being including:

- enhances strength, stamina and suppleness
- promotes a good mental attitude and discipline
- promotes defensive moves as opposed to aggression
- increases your awareness of danger
- increases body reflexes
- promotes a calmness of mind
- develops internal energy and power

clothing *and* equipment

In accordance with directives from *hombu* (headquarters) in Japan, adult students do not wear coloured belts, although the *kyu* (student) grading system still applies.

It is acceptable for children to wear coloured belts and the student system starts at 6th-*kyu*, which requires the wearing of a white belt with one red stripe. Children then progress through a number of coloured stripes and belts until they reach 1st-*kyu*, which is the final *kyu* grade before they are ready to take their black belt (lst-*dan*).

When students pass the examination for their 1st-*dan* (*shodan*), they are entitled to wear a *hakama* (a divided/pleated skirt). This is considered an honour and the grade is recorded at hombu. Students also receive a membership card, an international *yudansha* (*dan*-grade) record book and a certificate signed by the founder's son, Doshu (Kisshomaru Ueshiba).

Students who set an example or who work exceptionally hard for the benefit of the club i.e. administration, may be awarded permission to wear a hakama before they attain dan grade, subject to the senior instructor's discretion.

Smartly dressed with hakama tied correctly, prior to commencement of training.

black hakama

While practising aikido you will study the use of the bokken *(wooden sword), knife techniques and* jo *(a stick). This study is complementary to that of aikido. The* jo *should reach from the ground to just under the arm/shoulder, and it should be smooth and free from splinters for both safety and to allow free-flowing movements. The* bokken *or* bokuto *is a wooden sword made from Japanese oak (red or white), approximately the same size and shape as the sword (* katana*).*

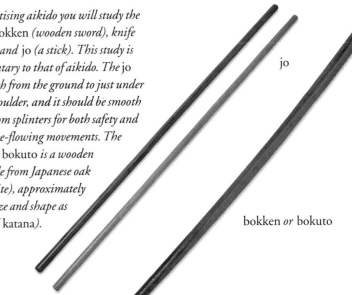

jo

bokken *or* bokuto

Etiquette

Aikido has strict codes of discipline and etiquette. These are necessary to ensure that the original spirit and attitude towards the art are maintained, with respect for the *dojo* and each other being observed at all times. A casual attitude towards training could result in injury. Care and courtesy should always be maintained.

RESPECTING THE FOUNDER – *In most traditional aikido dojos, it is very important to have a picture of the founder, Morihei Ueshiba. This may be positioned on the dojo floor, or on a table or wall, but it should be positioned centrally at the front of the dojo, or kamiza (meaning "seat of the Gods").*

❶ △ Sit facing the picture of Morihei Ueshiba in a kneeling position (*seiza*). Make sure your back is straight, feet are together and you are sitting on your heels. Your knees need to be about two fist-widths apart and, ideally, with the big toe of your right foot over the big toe of your left. Push your shoulders back and stay relaxed.

❷ △ Place your left hand in front of your body, with your fingers pushed together and your thumb forward, so that when the right hand meets the left they form a triangle.

❸ △ Bow deeply towards the *kamiza*. Make sure that your back is straight, and do not let your head touch the floor.

BOWING TO A PARTNER – *Demonstrating respect prior to practising with a partner.*

❶ △ When practising with a partner, the same form is followed. Sit opposite your partner, ensuring that there is a reasonable distance between you (usually an arm and a half). The bow (*rei*) is performed again, to show respect towards your partner. This seated bow is called *zarei*.

❷ △ Using the same hand and body positions as those in the bow (*rei*) to the *kamiza*, perform the bow towards your partner. Both partners bow simultaneously to show mutual respect.

THE BOW

Why, when and how to bow are natural questions raised by anyone taking up aikido. Most practitioners find that they soon adopt the custom and very quickly come to understand and enjoy the ritualized etiquette as an important part of their training process.

Correct etiquette is, above all, an expression of respect and courtesy to those with whom you are training. On entering the *dojo* (training room), perform a standing *rei* (bow) to the *kamiza* (desig-

nated area of respect where the instructor sits). Once you have asked, and been given permission to enter on to the mat (*tatami*) by the highest grade holder, perform a further standing *rei*. Practitioners then line up in a kneeling position, facing the *kamiza* in grade order: *kohei* (beginners) to the left of *sempai* (seniors), with the most senior on the right side of the *dojo*. You then wait until the class instructor comes on to the mat.

Exercise | Warm-up

Aikido, as with other martial arts, uses certain exercises to prepare the body for training and to ensure that muscles and tendons are warmed and stretched to avoid injury during practice. The exercises are designed to simultaneously stretch many areas of the body. Below are a selection that relate specifically to aikido.

WARM-UP 1 – *This exercise is performed on the legs, arms and torso, and is used to make the body more supple and relaxed. This is achieved through the gentle tapping action against the skin, which relaxes muscles and encourages blood to come to the surface of the skin.*

WARM-UP 2 – *After relaxing the body as in warm-up 1, you are ready to engage in stretching exercises. The following exercises continue to enhance blood circulation, while stretching the upper body.*

△ Place your right arm across your upper chest area and your left hand on your right elbow. Push your right arm as far around your body as you comfortably can, and half close your right fist. Starting at the back of the neck area, tap your body, working your way across the shoulder and down the arm.

△ With feet astride, drop the top half of your body forwards and swing your arms to either side. Keep your arms straight and look towards the arm that is moving in an upwards direction. This ensures that you fully stretch your body, in particular the waist, hips and arms.

WARM-UP 3 – *Inner thigh and hip exercise.*

◁ With your feet shoulder-width apart, lower your body, spreading your feet so that they face outwards. Place your elbows inside your knees with hands open and palms facing outwards. Gently push outwards to stretch your inner thighs. Repeat several times, trying to push a little further each time.

WARM-UP 4 – *Yoga type stretch and* tanden *(centre of gravity) exercise.*

❶ ◁ With your legs astride, as far apart as you can comfortably manage, lower your body, elbows together and fists clenched, cushioning your fore-head. It is very important to ensure that you have your elbows together, since this helps to stretch your upper body.

❷ △ Push your hands forwards and open them in preparation to bringing them around in a circular motion.

❸ △ As you push your hands forwards, have a feeling of using your stomach area (centre of gravity). It is a feeling of pushing your energy in a projected, forward motion. Bring your hands back into the centre position. Repeat this entire sequence 3 to 4 times.

Exercise | Loosening the neck

This exercise helps to loosen the muscles and tension in the back of the neck. The everyday stresses of life can cause tension and tightening in the back of the neck. Such tension can be relieved through the regular application of appropriate exercises. The following demonstrates one of the basic methods to enhance blood flow and stimulate muscles and tendons in the back of the neck.

◁ Place your right hand at the back of your neck, palm downwards and fingers pushed together. With the knife edge side of your hand, use a gentle "chopping" action, then gradually work up from the lower neck to the base of the skull, and then back down to the base. Repeat this exercise with your left hand on the opposite side of your neck.

Exercise | Kneeling practice

Kneeling techniques (*suwariwaza*) date back to the days of the *samurai*. Most aikido techniques can be practised from this position. Their primary purpose is to teach economy of movement and to make you aware of your *tanden* (centre) and hips. The techniques also promote flexibility in the lower limbs.

❶ △ Go down into a kneeling position with your left knee raised and your right knee lowered towards the floor. You should be on the balls of your feet with your heels close together. Keep your body upright with your hands forward as a defensive guard. Make sure you are looking forwards, not at the floor or around the *dojo*.

❷ △ Move forwards by placing the left knee down on to the floor and swivelling on it as you bring your right knee forwards. Swivel your knee and hips together to move forwards. This exercise is useful as a means of helping to develop the lower part of your body and is known as "walking on your knees" (*shikko*).

Exercise | Wrist flexibility

Many of the aikido techniques apply strong pressure to the wrist, elbow and shoulder joints. With great emphasis on fluent and supple movement, wrist exercises play an important part in the warm-up procedures. The exercises follow a prescribed technique, with each movement preparing the practitioner for the relevant method.

EXERCISE 1 – *The purpose of this exercise, known as* kote gaeshi *("wrist-out turn"), is to enhance the flexibility of your hands and wrists.*

△ Take hold of your left hand with your right hand. Push downwards and inwards in a twisting motion, pulling inwards towards your sternum. Ensure that your elbows are at about 90 degrees to your body and are horizontal. Repeat this exercise 2 or 3 times each side.

EXERCISE 3 – *This exercise is used in preparation for the technique called* shiho nage *or four-direction throw.*

❶ ◁ Take hold of your left hand at the centre of your body, with the palm of your right hand on top of the back of your left, fingers facing upwards. Keep your hands close to your chest and ensure that your elbows are down and arms tucked in close to your body. The elbow forms the fulcrum of this exercise.

❷ ◁ Using a rotating action towards the outer part of your body, start to turn your fingertips in a downwards, circular motion. Then rotate your wrist about your elbow. Apply gentle pressure on the left hand to stretch the forearms, elbows and wrists. This relaxes the elbow and enhances flexibility of your lower arm. Repeat this exercise 2 to 3 times each side.

EXERCISE 2 – *Preparation for* sankyo *wrist techniques. Sankyo is a painful, but very effective wrist restraint.*

 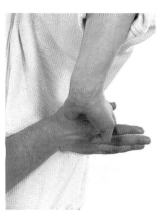

❶ △ Turn your left hand slightly inwards with your fingertips pointing towards your abdomen. This exercise has been developed in preparation for a technique known as *sankyo*. Prepare for the grip, using your right hand to turn your left hand inwards so that your knuckles are facing towards your chest.

❷ △ Twist and turn your wrist to the left side to ensure maximum rotation of the lower arm and wrist. Release and repeat the exercise with the right hand. Your hand needs to be well drawn in and move in an inward, circular motion, to apply pressure on the ligaments in your forearm.

EXERCISE 4 – *This exercise is in preparation for the technique called* nikkyo *or "wrist-in turn".*

△ Cover the back of your left hand with your right hand. Pull in towards the solar plexus area. This exercise assists in loosening and strengthening the wrist area.

Exercise | Spiritual development

Aikido seeks to develop your spiritual side in order to promote your inner calm. The attainment of inner tranquility is fundamental to clearing and focusing the mind in all aspects of life. The following exercises seek to bring together the qualities of correct breathing, known as *kokkyo* (breath power), as part of the spiritual development of aikido.

ROWING EXERCISE – *TORIFUNE* – *Think of this rowing exercise as a way of "rowing" from this world to the next. The exercise starts slowly but, towards the end of the session, the tempo is increased as you move "closer to Utopia". In the physical dimension it is used as a centering technique to instill a feeling of good body posture and, by emphasizing hip movement, to increase the awareness of your own centre of gravity.*

❶ ◁ Stand in the upright posture known as *migi hanmi* – right foot forward. *Migi* is Japanese for "right" and *hanmi* means "posture". Lean forwards and feel a sense of pressure from the hips. Fully extend your hands and start a rowing action, as if in a boat with oars.

❷ ◁ Pull back your fists to your hips, with your elbows tucked in, and around 70 per cent of your weight on your rear leg. Repeat this action several times and then change leg positions and repeat. Breathing is very important in this exercise – exhale on the forward movement using the sound of "*hei*" and, as you move back with your fists to the hip position, inhale, then exhale, using a "*ho*" sound. This is a low sound, which comes from the pit of the abdomen.

CALMING EXERCISE – *FURITAMA* – *This exercise is designed to bring an overall feeling of calmness to the body.*

❶ △ Stand in a relaxed position with your feet a shoulder-width apart. Fully extend your arms at the sides, palms upwards and with fingers open – as if grasping energy from the universe. Keep your eyes closed to maintain a feeling of calm.

❷ △ Bring your hands together, palms touching, above your head, with your fingers pointing upwards.

❸ △ Next, bring your hands down in front of your body in the region of your lower abdomen. Clasp your hands together, using a shaking motion, as if vibrating a heavy ball in your abdomen. The shaking movement is designed to help disperse the energy you have throughout your body.

Exercise | Breathing

In aikido, correct breathing not only oxygenates the blood, but also stimulates certain internal organs. In order to generate *kokkyo* (breath power), it is necessary to breathe deeply, with the emphasis on abdominal expansion and contraction, as opposed to simply breathing through the chest cavity. The following demonstrates just one of the many techniques we can learn.

❶ ◁ Stretch your body, arms above your head, with your palms facing upwards. As you perform this exercise, breathe in through your nose, imagining the breath going up to the top of your head, down the spine and into the centre of your abdomen. Perform this exercise slowly and deeply, as if there were a coil within your body, gradually unwinding. It may help to imagine that you have a spring in your abdomen – as you inhale it is compressed and as you exhale it is allowed to expand.

❷ △ As you bend at the waist to lower your body, begin to exhale.

❸ △ Try to touch your knees with your forehead by clasping the back of your ankles to pull your body inwards. At the same time, exhale fully. As you return to the original standing position, inhale then exhale as you remain standing. Repeat this exercise several times.

Exercise | Back-stretching

Traditional aikido places great emphasis on having a supple spine. Back-stretching exercises are, therefore, very much a part of every warm-up and cool-down session. The following exercises focus primarily on back-stretching and have benefits for the whole body in terms of flexibility and fitness.

EXERCISE 1 – *Sotai-dosa (paired practice) back-stretching exercise.*

❶ △ With feet shoulder-width apart, step forward into a natural right foot posture. As your partner takes hold of your wrists, extend your fingers and imagine you have a sword in your hands.

❷ △ Using a circular motion, bring your right foot forwards and upwards, approximately 45 degrees in front of your partner. Twist your body 180 degrees with the feeling that you are now cutting with the sword as you turn to the rear. You will then be back-to-back with your partner.

❸ ◁ Keep turning your body as if you are cutting with your sword across your partner's throat. Both partners need to work together to gain benefit from this exercise. Hold your partner in this position for 5–6 seconds and then change roles, before repeating the exercise to the opposite side.

▽ Your partner at this point should have a very arched back and be gripping your arm for support, as you can see below, in this alternative view of this same position.

EXERCISE 2 – Ganseki otoshi *(head over heels throw). This is an effective defence used as a back-stretching exercise.*

1 △ Your partner moves in with an overhead strike to the top of your head. Come in to meet the strike with your right forearm. In this exercise, this is purely a defensive move, although the defender treats the strike as a committed attack.

2 △ With your right foot forward, bring your left foot around and pivot on the ball of your right foot so that you are now behind your partner. Maintain arm contact as you prepare for the next stage.

3 △ Take hold of your partner's collar at the back of the neck with your left hand, while pushing your right arm and elbow into the centre of your partner's back in preparation for the lift.

4 △ Once you feel secure, with your arm well positioned in the small of your partner's back, drop into a very low posture, keeping your knees well bent. *Note: while this is only an exercise, it must be performed with care and caution at all stages.*

5 ▷ Gently lift your partner off the floor so that their body is completely arched and relaxed. The purpose of this exercise is to offer your partner support by using your body underneath to lift and gently bounce as your partner relaxes. Hold this position for approximately 15–20 seconds then change sides and repeat once only.

EXERCISE 3 – Ushiro ryote *(rear attack, both wrists held). Here, actual defence techniques are used as a back-stretch.*

❶ △ Your partner approaches from the rear and grabs hold of both of your wrists.

❷ △ Start to move by bringing your right arm directly above your head to pull your partner off balance.

❸ △ Turn completely around, moving towards your partner at the same time. You should now be facing your partner, who must still hold on to your wrists in preparation for the back-stretching exercise. It is important to work cooperatively to ensure the success of this exercise.

❹ △ Your partner's back will now be fully arched. Their body must stay relaxed. You must maintain a good, strong, upright posture in order to support your partner. *Note: maintain this position for no more than 10 seconds, especially when first learning this exercise. Gently allow your partner to move back to an upright position.*

EXERCISE 4 – *Another defence technique that can be used as a warm-up stretch for your partner.*

1 △ Your partner takes hold of both of your wrists.

2 △ Start to move in with your right foot, pulling your left foot inwards. At the same time, bring your right arm across your partner's chest, keeping your left arm fully extended and forward.

3 ▷ Slowly push your arm downwards and across the area of your partner's neck. With the twist of your hips, by following this movement through, you can throw your partner. *Note: do not apply any pressure to the neck. This is an exercise purely to promote suppleness. Hold position for 5–10 seconds and repeat.*

Technique | Basic stance and posture

Aikido adopts the back triangle stance (*ura-sankaku*). The triangle shape is achieved by the positioning of the feet. This is the only posture from which the *tanden* (centre) can be held effectively when executing a technique, and from where rapid movement in any direction is possible.

❶ ◁ Align the heels of both feet, with your front foot facing forwards and slightly outwards, and your rear foot at an angle of 60 degrees. Bend your knees slightly and place about 60 per cent of your weight on your front leg. Keep your hands in the guard position to protect your body. This stance is known as *hanmi* (half stance).

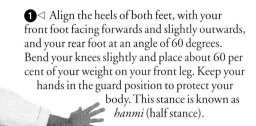

△Ideally the heel of your front foot must be in line with the heel of your rear foot, in a triangular shape, like being on a tight rope.

❷ △ In this overview, the 180 degree turn (*tenkan*) is being demonstrated. This is the continual turning movement to assist in the flowing techniques used in aikido. With the left foot forwards, turn on the ball of the foot and bring the left foot around circularly.

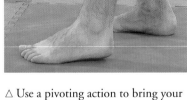

△ Use a pivoting action to bring your left leg around in a circular motion towards the rear. This detailed close-up shows the correct feet position in preparation for the turn.

❸ ◁ After pivoting, you will have smoothly turned completely around 180 degrees and will be facing in the opposite direction, with your right foot forward. Depending on whether you use the front or rear foot to initiate the movement will dictate which foot is forward on the final turn. Qualified supervision is required to practise.

NOTE

In aikido each partner is referred to as the *uke* or *tori*. The **uke** is the initial attacker who will "receive" the restraint or throw and the *tori* will "execute" the defensive technique .

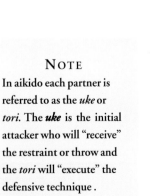

Technique | Standing

Learning to defend from a variety of different angles is important. The following demonstrates the use of the wrist technique *sankyo*, during an attack called *yoko menuchi* – a roundhouse strike to the side of the head. This is a very effective restraint from which it is difficult for an aggressor to escape.

1 △ Your partner comes in with a *yoko menuchi* technique, which is similar to a bottle being swung around to the side of the head. You defend yourself against the attack by coming in to meet the technique and deflect it with your left hand, while placing your right hand in front of your partner's face as a distraction.

2 ▽ Using a large circular motion, step through with your left foot as if walking through your partner. Keep the upward circular motion going, and then pull your partner's right hand back with your right hand, ensuring that their palm is facing outwards, while applying pressure on their elbow joint with your left hand.

3 ◁ Step through with your left leg, into a deep stance. Change the grip by moving your left hand down to take a secure hold of your partner's right hand. Keep your body in close and lean forwards to ensure that your left shoulder is well in to the side of your partner. From here there are a variety of final techniques that can be applied to fully restrain.

Technique | *Ikkyo – Suwari-waza*

Ikkyo is the first principle in arm pinning techniques and mastery of it is required to understand subsequent methods and skills. It can be practised from any attack, whether kneeling (*suwari-waza*), as shown here, or standing (*tachi-waza*). Sitting and standing practice is referred to as *hanmi-handachi*.

CAUTION

Never continue with a technique in which your partner is face down – this is dangerous and can cause asphyxiation. Always ensure that your partner has an arm free to tap the ground if the technique is being applied too heavily. Your partner should feel only enough pressure to ensure that the movement has been properly applied.

❶ ▷ Your partner comes at you with an overhead strike to the top of your head. This is known as *shomen uchi* and can be executed with the open hand or with the use of a weapon such as a knife. Defend by using both hands in an upwards motion to meet the attacking arm. *Note: use minimal aggression – a flowing motion and circular action have more impact than a static movement.*

❷ ▽ The twisting and turning action of the movement will help to bring your partner to the floor. This demonstrates the force that can be successfully applied. *Note: it is important that your partner is well experienced in break-falling techniques, to perform the technique as depicted. If not, you must gently position your partner in preparation for the final restraining technique.*

❸ △ The final pin is effective by holding above the elbow and wrist, making sure the arm is slightly higher than the shoulder. Push from the centre of gravity with a twisting action.

Technique | *Kotegaeshi*

Kotegaeshi (wrist-out turn) is a basic technique whereby the defender places his hand on the back of the attacker's hand and applies pressure in two ways – inwards to break the power in attacking wrist and arm, and outwards to cause the attacker to fall onto their back, prior to restraining.

❶ △ As your partner moves in with the overhead attack, move in and underneath to meet the attack with your right forearm. Your left arm is to the side and ready to go over your partner's right arm. Start to draw your hands downwards towards your partner's wrist, simultaneously keeping the momentum of the circle going towards you, and prepare to swing your body round to the left side.

❷ ◁ Take hold of your partner's right wrist to bring her arm down towards your thighs. This is important, since this is part of a flowing, continuous movement that uses your partner's energy as well as your own.

❸ ▽ Continue the circular movement in the opposite direction. The complete motion is almost like a figure eight, with your partner's fingers being bent back to face downwards.

❹ ▷ Move through with your left knee, maintaining a firm grip on your partner's wrist, while securing pressure on your partner's elbow joint. As your partner feels they are about to hit the floor, continue the circle towards your left side by bringing your left knee around and both hands downwards in the same direction. This will force your partner to roll onto their back.

△ A locking technique showing the firm control required to immobilize your partner.

Technique | *Kata dori*

Kata dori is a shoulder grasp with one hand while the aggressor strikes with the other or kicks. The grasping arm is stretched sideways to take the attacker's balance prior to execution of the technique. This technique is also a useful self-defence move against clothing being grabbed in the street.

❶ △ Your partner moves in and grabs you by the sleeve.

❷ ▷ Bring your right hand across your partner's attacking right arm. Start to move your body forwards with your left foot so that you can start to pull your partner off balance.

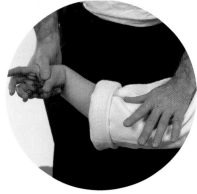

△ To move into step 3, bring your left hand under your partner's right elbow, with your palm open and fingers upright. Bring your right hand under their wrist to apply a large circular forwards and downwards motion so that their right arm is in front of you.

△ To apply this alternative arm lock, place your left hand on your partner's elbow and your right hand on her wrist. Next, with your right hand, twist your partner's right hand with their fingers pointing away from you. Maintain pressure on the elbow joint.

△ A wrist technique such as *sankyo* can also be applied as an alternative manoeuvre. Pull your partner's left arm backwards and inward. This will cause the ligaments and nerves to twist.

❸ ◁ Continue to step forwards to completely take your partner off balance and slide your left arm down towards their right thumb. This is in preparation to secure a wrist lock.

❹ △ Apply a wrist lock by placing your left hand on the elbow joint to secure the restraint.

❺ △ Maintain the wrist lock by taking hold of your partner's hand. Make sure their fingers are facing upwards.

❻ ▷ Using a circular motion, bring your partner's right hand upwards, with her fingers pointing towards your face. This technique will cause discomfort and she may well come up on to her toes to release the pressure. This demonstrates that the technique has been correctly applied. Do not continue to apply pressure and release the hold as soon as possible.

Technique | Rear defence

Aikido incorporates defence from any attack, including holds or strikes from behind. Attacks from the rear are called *ushiro waza* (rear techniques). The following is an example of *ushiro katate dori kubeshime* (rear strangle with one hand held), demonstrating the effective use of posture and stance to support the technique being applied.

❶ ▷You are grabbed from behind, around the throat, by your partner's right arm, and your left wrist is held by their left hand.

❷ △ Step back with your left leg, going underneath the attack. Project your energy forwards to take your attacker off balance. From this position a variety of techniques can be applied, as in step 3 below.

❸ △ In this case, apply a wrist lock to restrain your partner. Place your left hand on top of their left hand and your right hand on their wrist. Pull her hand to your chest and twist her fingers outwards, towards your right side. This action will cause the ligaments and nerves to twist.

Technique | Front defence

The following demonstrates a defence against a two-handed strangle known as *udehishige* (arm smashing). This technique is one of the few transmitted from *daito-ryu-ju-jitsu* that has not been changed from its original form. The founder modified many of the original techniques to incorporate his philosophy of *"aiki"*, making them less destructive.

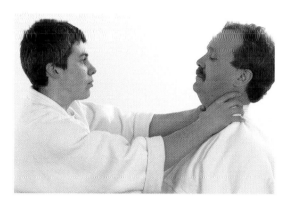

❶ △ You are grabbed by your partner around the throat from the front. Ideally, you need to start your defensive action before the grab is secure, but if this is not possible there are various techniques taught in aikido to defeat the attack.

❷ ▷ Practise this technique with the aim of taking hold of your partner's right wrist before contact is made.

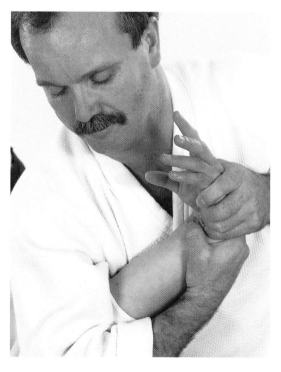

❸ △ Once you have grabbed your partner, bring your right arm over her arm, at the same time grabbing her right hand with your left hand and, simultaneously, twisting your body forwards to execute a lock on her arm, wrist and hand. The tips of your partner's fingers need to be pointing backwards.

❹ ▷ Twist your body around as far as you can away from your partner. Keep the lock close to your body, however. This will ensure an effective restraint or, alternatively, you can release your partner, projecting her forwards as part of a take down technique. Once the armlock is established, apply pressure by twisting your hips to the right.

Technique | Women's self-defence

While this section is referred to as "women's self-defence", the same techniques are also used by men and children. Aikido, being based upon the principle of the circle and using the aggressor's force, means that regardless of the size of the aggressor, your body weight can be used to maximize your advantage.

SHIHO NAGE – Four-direction throw – once the elbow is controlled it is possible to throw an attacker forwards, backwards or to either side.

❶ △ The attacker pins the arms to the side from behind, affecting a hug. Step forwards and extend your arms outwards in order to avoid encirclement.

❷ △ Extend your arms outwards with your right arm moving upwards and left arm in a downwards direction. With your left hand take hold of your partner's left wrist.

❸ △ Maintain the circular momentum as you step back and throw your partner forwards. Keep your body calm and extend your energy as you move through and throw.

IRIMI NAGE – This technique means "entering body throw".

❶ △ An aggressor tries to deliver a punch to your chest or stomach. Side-step to your left with your left foot to avoid it and deflect the aggressor's right-handed punch. This is an evasive technique. You can use your left hand (palm heel) to deflect the attack, but the most important thing is to move your body to the side so that you can deliver an immediate counter-attack. Once you have avoided the attack, bring your right hand up and across in a large circular action as you step through with your right foot. Simultaneously, bring your right arm under the aggressor's jaw line in preparation for a throw.

❷ △ Moving through, well into the aggressor's space, and breaking his posture, will cause him to lose balance and succumb to your technique. This requires minimal force but needs calmness, a flowing action, good timing and continuous movement.

ADVANCED
Technique | Self-defence against a knife

The category for knife defences is known as *tanto* or *tanken dori*. The aikido principle is still to evade the attack and use the aggressor's force against them. The knife is kept at a distance, while the flowing defensive manoeuvres are applied, utilizing the aggressor's energy to work in your favour.

CAUTION

When learning defences against a weapon attack it is vital to have qualified supervision and to practise in a safe environment. Never practise with a real weapon when you are learning, especially in the early stages. Wooden or plastic knives are ideal, but you still need to treat them with respect – any item can be dangerous if it is used incorrectly.

❶ ▷ As the aggressor comes in with a right-handed knife attack to your stomach area, move to your left and block the strike with the outside edge of your hand. If, however, the attacker is left-handed, it would be more appropriate to move to your right. Bring the left foot forwards into a movement known as *irimi tenkan*, which is a 180-degree turn. It requires you to move in towards your opponent, turning your body, and the circular action and the physical movement will bring your opponent with you. You are turning outside your opponent's attacking energy, which is the principle of *tenkan*.

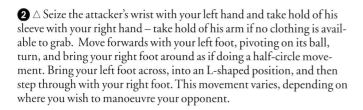

❷ △ Seize the attacker's wrist with your left hand and take hold of his sleeve with your right hand – take hold of his arm if no clothing is available to grab. Move forwards with your left foot, pivoting on its ball, turn, and bring your right foot around as if doing a half-circle movement. Bring your left foot across, into an L-shaped position, and then step through with your right foot. This movement varies, depending on where you wish to manoeuvre your opponent.

❸ △ Twist underneath the attacking arm and into a large circular movement, using your hands to take the aggressor off balance. As the aggressor enters into your movement, he is spun around – an action responsible for many of the dynamic throws employed in aikido. The force of the fall should ensure that he drops the knife. If appropriate, you could also apply a restraining hold, depending on the circumstances. If the attacker still has the knife, apply a further restraint to remove the weapon.

Technique | Throwing – Nage waga

The following shows one of the basic throwing techniques to be found in aikido called *kaiten-nage*. As with all aikido styles, *kaiten-nage* seeks to develop the skills of both practitioners. The defender is learning the mechanics of the movement, as the partner also learns to use their agility to roll out of the throwing technique.

KAITEN-NAGE – *Objective is to spin your partner on to his back.*

> ### CAUTION
> As with all advanced techniques, especially throwing, it is very important for both partners to be experienced in break-falling before attempting any of these techniques.

❶ ▷ An aggressor comes in with a punch to your solar plexus. You side-step and block with your right arm, bringing your left hand across to the back of the aggressor's neck. This technique is called *kaiten-nage*, which means "spin throw".

❷ △ Next, pull the aggressor's head down towards the floor with your left hand, while simultaneously pushing the aggressor's left arm upwards with your right hand. *Note: keep an upright, well-centred posture.*

❸ ▷ Finally, apply a throwing technique by pushing the aggressor's left arm forwards.

The following are some of the moves and techniques practised when using weapons such as the *bokken* and *jo*. Various *kata* (sequences of set moves) are taught, with and without a training partner, not only to develop skills in the use of weapons, but also to give a greater understanding of posture, timing and applications of *ma-ai* (combative distance).

1 △ As the attacker thrusts with a *bokken*, the defender comes up underneath with their *bokken* to block the oncoming attack, prior to cutting the aggressor.

2 △ The defender brings the *bokken* around his head and strikes the aggressor on the side of the neck.

▷ Demonstrating, using the *jo*, a technique called *otoshi tsuki* (meaning "drop thrust").

Exercise | Cool-down

Aikido practitioners believe it is important to cool down at the end of a session. One partner takes the other on to their back and gently extends upwards and outwards – the idea being to relax worked muscles and stretch the spine, to prevent stiffness ensuing after practice. The following moves demonstrate just two of a variety of body-relaxing exercises.

COOL-DOWN 1 – Haishin undo *(back stretching)*

❶ ◁ Your partner takes hold of both your wrists.

❷ ▷ Turn underneath and completely around, while your partner maintains a hold on your wrists, so that you are now back to back.

❸ ▷ Drop your body down and place your buttocks well under your partner's buttocks in preparation for the lift. Lift your partner up and across your back, stretching your arms forwards. It is important that your partner totally relaxes while you gently stretch forward to loosen their spine. *Note: this exercise must not be performed if either of you have any back problems. If in doubt, consult a doctor.*

COOL-DOWN 2 – *Another interesting, unique technique in aikido is using the* bokken *in the cool-down exercises.*

❶ △ A similar cool-down technique uses the *bokken*. Stand facing each other in the standard *hanmi* posture. Your partner takes hold of your right wrist with both hands.

❷ △ Turn to the side with your right foot and pivot completely around on your left foot in an anticlockwise (counterclockwise) direction by bringing your right leg to the rear. At the same time, raise the *bokken* as if to start to cut.

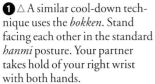

❸ ▷ Continue the turn so that you are now facing the opposite direction and bring the *bokken* above your head as you turn. This will lift your partner and bring her across your back. Hold for 15 to 20 seconds and change sides. Perform this exercise slowly and carefully.

JU-JITSU

Ju-jitsu is an effective self-defence system used extensively by the military and police forces around the world. Special features of the art include defences against knife attacks and immobilizing techniques. Another unique skill taught to highly qualified practitioners is the art of resuscitation. This technique, known as *kuatsu,* was developed on the battlefield where, following the delivery of a non-fatal ju-jitsu technique, rather than deliver a final killing blow, a Japanese *samurai* would revive the injured enemy for questioning.

JU-JITSU

柔術

history *and* philosophy

The art of ju-jitsu is interpreted as being the "science of softness". Translated literally, *ju* means "gentle" or "soft" and *jitsu* means "art". While referred to as "a gentle art" some of the techniques are, nevertheless, extremely dynamic in their delivery and would appear to be anything but soft.

There are many stories regarding the origins of ju-jitsu, dating as far back as the 8th century, with historical lines indicating roots even before the time of Christ. While some people claim that ju-jitsu originated in China, the ancient chronicles of Japan describe how, in AD 712, Tatemi Kazuchi threw Tatemi Nokami, like "throwing a leaf". Reference is also made in the *Nihon Sho-ki* chronicles to the Emperor Shuinjin holding a martial arts tournament to celebrate the seventh year of his reign in 23 BC. One of the bouts resulted in the death of a participant, a sumo wrestler, who was thrown to the ground and kicked by Nomino Sukume. These accounts provide evidence of early "empty-hand" techniques in Japan. There is also reference to ju-jitsu developing as an art from the work of a Buddhist monk, dating back to the 13th century. These ancient techniques were known as *kumi-tachi* (or *yawara*), which is described in the *Konjaku-monogatari*, a Buddhist work dating back to that time.

A few practitioners of ju-jitsu choose to keep alive the warrior spirit of the fighting techniques.

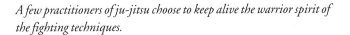

The samurai *(also known as* bushi*), wearing colourful and elaborate armour.*

Another reference to a ju-jitsu-like form of combat is found in the 15th-century martial art tradition known as the katori-shinto ryu. It is believed, however, that ju-jitsu was brought to Japan by a Chinese monk called Chen Yuanein (1587-1671). So, although ju-jitsu is viewed today as a Japanese martial art, there is strong evidence pointing to Chinese origins.

While ju-jitsu was first practised in Japan by the *samurai*, followed by the *ninja*, it inevitably spread further afield and was, sadly, embraced by many of the bandits of the time.

Through this dubious association, ju-jitsu earned a poor reputation. It was during this time that Jiguro Kano developed the art of judo, meaning "the gentle way", from a combination of ju-jitsu techniques. His aim was to correct the reputation ju-jitsu had acquired as a deadly art through its connections with banditry.

What is ju-jitsu?

The central philosophy behind ju-jitsu is to conquer an opponent by any and all means – as long as minimal force

Ju-jitsu followers conform to a strict discipline – both mental and physical.

The essence of ju-jitsu is the power of resistance and effective timing.

only is used. Consequently, this precept demands from its followers a strict conformity to various disciplines – both mental and physical.

Physical fitness has always been a fundamental prerequisite for practitioners of ju-jitsu. A characteristic of this art involves strict moral and dietary regimes, which are seen as being necessary if one is to reach the highest level of perfection. It is therefore not surprising that, historically, many ju-jitsu masters withdrew to religious institutions, such as Buddhist or Shinto shrines.

Although the fundamental principle behind modern ju-jitsu as a self-defence art is to conquer an opponent using minimal force, the older art of ju-jitsu focused on literally annihilating the enemy, which led to the development of many dangerous and fatal techniques.

Warrior traditions

The *samurai* followed a strict code of discipline called the *bushido* – the "way of the warrior". This code included such concepts as loyalty, duty, obedience, honour and respect. The code influenced not just their behaviour in battle, but their daily lives, too. This would become the basis of the Zen Buddhist philosophy – reaching for salvation within, rather

than turning to a monument or god. The *samurai* believed that man could influence his own destiny, especially when faced with warfare and possible death – a concept which certainly appealed to them.

The traditional art of ju-jitsu is still carried on today by a minority of practitioners, who wish to keep alive the warrior spirit of the deadly fighting techniques of the art. They do not enter competitions and their only goal is the continuation of the mental, spiritual and physical purity of the art.

BENEFITS OF JU-JITSU

The principal benefits that derive from learning the art of ju-jitsu include:

- **Fitness and flexibility**
- **Confidence and well-being**
- **Self-defence skills**
- **Assertiveness and awareness**
- **Stress reduction**
- **Comradeship**
- **Self-discipline and a positive attitude**

clothing *and* equipment

In ju-jitsu students generally wear a white suit (*gi*) and a red belt. This depicts their beginner status. They will then follow the grade system, changing belt colours as they achieve each grade detailed below. When students attain their first black belt grade (1st-*dan – shodan*) their clothing is changed to a black jacket and white trousers, which can become a blue jacket from 4th-*dan*. It is always important to ensure that the suit fits comfortably for safety and practicality. It is also necessary that students and instructors keep their suits in good repair and are always smart in appearance. Personal hygiene is very important, particularly when practising in close proximity with another partner. Practitioners must ensure that their nails are clean and short, that jewellery is removed and hair is tied back where appropriate. This is important, as there are many close proximity techniques in ju-jitsu, and this will avoid unnecessary injury. It is compulsory in this style of ju-jitsu for both men and women to wear groin protection (athletic cup) from the day they begin their training.

gi *top*

groin protection (athletic cup)

trousers

zori

BELT GRADINGS

7th-*kyu*	White (red stripe)
6th-*kyu*	Yellow
5th-*kyu*	Orange
4th-*kyu*	Green
3rd-*kyu*	Blue
2nd-*kyu*	Purple
1st-*kyu*	Brown
Shodan-ho	Black and brown (provisional black)
1st–5th-*dan*	Black
6th-*dan* and upwards	Red and white

red belt   *white belt*   *yellow belt*   *orange belt*   *green belt*   *blue belt*

purple belt   *brown belt*   *black/brown belt*   *black belt*   *red/white belt*

Equipment

The *hojo jutsu* rope is unique to the art of ju-jitsu. It was originally used by the *samurai* to detain prisoners of war as part of their duty when they served as feudal police. Today, around the world, the *hojo jutsu* rope is still used by many police and special security forces to detain criminals, prisoners and terrorists. Below is a selection of the weapons used in ju-jitsu. There are many other weapons, such as the *hoko* and *yari* (spears), *naginata* (wooden staff) and *nunchaku* (small rice flail).

A hakama is also worn in ju-jitsu usually for the specific practise of certain techniques and for demonstrations.

jo

bo

kamma

sai

tanto

hojo jutsu *rope*

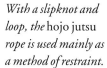

With a slipknot and loop, the hojo jutsu *rope is used mainly as a method of restraint.*

tonfa

Etiquette

Etiquette is important as a sign of respect to the spirit of the art (*shomen*), instructors, students and to the training environment (*dojo*). This form of etiquette is an integral part of the practice. The following demonstrates the kneeling bow (*rei*) followed by the standing bow, before commencing training.

KNEELING *REI* (BOW)

1 △ Lower yourself down on to your left knee with both hands towards your left hip. This position represents holding a sword as in the day of the Japanese *samurai*.

2 △ Take hold of your trousers with your right hand on your right knee. (This movement represents the *samurai* wearing the *hakama* – pleated trousers/skirt, and the need to slightly lift this garment before drawing the foot in.) Bring your right foot back so as not to compromise your stance in the event that you need to quickly respond to an attack.

3 △ Bring your right leg back so that you can lower your body to sit on both heels with your feet flat. Position your hands at the top of your thighs and keep your arms and shoulders relaxed. Make sure your knees are no more than two fists apart. It is disrespectful for your knees to be any wider than this. Place your hands on the tops of your thighs with your fingers pushed together. Continue to look forwards with your back and shoulders in an upright position. Although this is an assertive position, keep your body relaxed.

4 △ Prior to performing the *rei*, there is a rather more assertive posture in the form of a slight "snap" action. As you start to bow forwards, place your left hand to the front of your body. This depicts protecting the sword, which would be carried on the left side of the body. While being a sign of respect, it is also a sign of possible distrust. Overall, the etiquette needs to be performed smoothly and naturally.

5 △ Follow through with your right hand, making sure that your fingers and thumb touch to make a diamond shape – this is known as the *kongo zen* diamond. This side view of the bow shows the correct angle of the head, hands and feet.

STANDING *REI* (BOW)

▷ Following the kneeling bow, come back into the kneeling position and stand up, stepping forwards with your right foot, then the left. With your heels together and feet at a 45 degree angle, keep your hands flat to your sides in line with the seams of your trousers. Look forwards with an assertive manner. From this position, lower the top part of your body from the waist, approximately 30 degrees, and then move back into the starting position. You are now ready to commence your ju-jitsu practice.

Exercise | Warm-up

It is very important to carry out appropriate warm-up exercises before beginning ju-jitsu practice. These usually consist of running around the outside of the *dojo* to loosen up your body and increase your heart rate, improving circulation. The running exercise can incorporate a variety of physical moves as part of the warm-up routine.

WARM-UP 1 – *This exercise will loosen your shoulder muscles and joints.*

❶ ◁ With feet a shoulder-width apart, rotate both your arms in a forwards, circular motion.

❹ ◁ Push your right arm upwards, as if to touch your left shoulder. This will apply gentle pressure to your elbow joint and increase suppleness. Repeat this movement with your left arm 2 or 3 times.

❷ △ Here you can see the arms going above the head, continuing the circular action to the rear and then returning to the start position. Use a large, circular action at a medium pace only. Repeat this exercise several times and then reverse the action so that your arms are moving backwards and then forwards.

❸ △ With your feet a shoulder-width apart, cross your arms in front of your body by bringing your left arm on top of your right arm.

WARM-UP 2 – *This exercise will help forearm development.*

❶ ◁ Stretch out your right hand in front of your body with your palm facing outwards. Keep your fingers tightly closed together and your thumb tucked in.

△ This close-up shows the correct position of your hands.

❷ ◁ With your left hand, take hold of the back of your right hand. Ensure your left thumb is placed on top of your right hand. Again, your fingers need to be pushed together.

❸ ▷ Pull your right hand in towards your nose or chin area. This will stimulate a pulling sensation to the forearm muscles and tendons. Maintain pressure with a slight twisting action. Relax and repeat 3 or 4 times. Repeat with the left hand.

WARM-UP 3 – *A series of easy exercises designed to loosen up your hips and knees and to stretch your leg muscles.*

❶ ◁ Standing with your feet a shoulder-width apart, place your hands on your hips and start to rotate them in a clockwise direction. Make sure you keep your feet firmly flat on the ground and that you are working the middle part of your body. This exercise is particularly good for the base of the spine and pelvis.

❷ ▷ With your feet together, bend your knees. Place the palm of your hands on top of your knees and push in a circular clockwise direction. Repeat several times. Then repeat the exercise in an anticlockwise (counterclockwise) direction. Perform this movement slowly and gently to increase the suppleness of your knees, without causing cartilage problems.

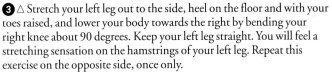

❸ △ Stretch your left leg out to the side, heel on the floor and with your toes raised, and lower your body towards the right by bending your right knee about 90 degrees. Keep your left leg straight. You will feel a stretching sensation on the hamstrings of your left leg. Repeat this exercise on the opposite side, once only.

❹ △ Start with feet shoulder-width apart and step forwards. Place your hands on your hips, turn to your right and push forwards with your right knee. Ensure that your left leg remains straight with your heel firmly on the floor. Push forwards with your hips to stretch the tendons of the left leg. Your chest should be upwards and forwards, chin up and eyes looking forwards. Repeat this exercise to the left side once only.

❶ ◁ Stand with your feet a shoulder-width apart and turn them outwards, as if rocking on the outside edges of your feet.

❷ ◁ Pull your knees inwards and transfer your weight on to the inside edges of your feet in a rolling action.

▽ Roll on to the sides of your feet as shown here, as far as you comfortably can.

▽ Roll on to your instep.

❸ ◁ Straighten your legs and roll your weight forwards, so that you are balancing on the balls of your feet.

❹ ◁ Roll your weight backwards so you are balancing on your heels. Keep your arms forward to maintain good balance. Repeat 3 or 4 times each side.

▽ Keep your heels well raised for maximum benefit.

▽ Keep toes curled upwards and off the floor.

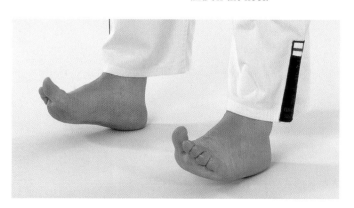

Technique | Blocking

There are various defensive techniques in ju-jitsu that involve blocking, covering the head, upper body and lower body. The following techniques demonstrate some of these blocks. There are comparative blocking techniques which can be found in other martial arts such as karate and tae kwondo. The blocks here are particular to ju-jitsu.

S BLOCK – *Swan neck block*

❶ ◁ Face your partner with your left hand forward, assuming a guard position.

❷ ▷ As your partner moves towards you with a round-house punch (right hook) to the head, turn your body to the left and bring your left arm forwards through the centre of your body and out towards the left. Following this S block, you would make a strike to the face, body or groin area. Make sure that your palm is facing downwards with your fingers locked together. Repeat this exercise, reversing roles with your partner.

❸ ▷ As you move through with the S block, prepare your right hand, ready to strike your partner.

◁ This close-up demonstrates the effectiveness of the S block.

❹ ▽ With your right hand palm heel, aim to strike towards your partner's chin, focusing your strike at least 3–5 in (7.5–13 cm) away from your partner's chin. This is important to maintain safety. *Note: blocking will incur contact, but be sensible in the delivery of your techniques.*

❶ △ Move into a formal posture (left-hand fighting stance) with about three-quarters of your weight on your back leg. This enables you to use your front leg in a rapid kicking technique, should this be necessary – or any other defensive technique.

❷ ◁ As your partner moves towards you with a right-fist strike at your head, step across and block with both hands. Ensure that your left hand is in the "open-hand" position.

▽ Keep looking at your partner when performing your techniques and do not drop your guard.

❸ ◁ Grab your partner's right wrist and prepare to strike. It is important to adopt a strong posture, while you bring your fist across your body, before delivering the strike.

❹ ▽ Strike your partner in the float-ing rib with the side of your right fist (hammer fist). Your fingers should be tightly clenched with your thumb locked over the top of your fingers.

▷ Maintain a secure grip while striking.

❺ △ Depending on the situation, you can now apply an arm lock. When doing this it is important to aim for the weak areas of your partner's body. Your right arm must clasp your partner's right arm just above the elbow joint, your left hand securing his wrist. *Note that your right foot is positioned behind your part-ner's right foot. This gives good posture and stance and ensures that your partner cannot follow through with any further movements.*

110

ADVANCED
Technique | Shoulder lock

The following demonstrates a combination of blocking, striking and locking techniques that can be used to restrain an aggressor. This sequence of moves is typical of many ju-jitsu techniques, which combine the hard and soft concept. Each move in itself may be applied from different directions and can have several variations.

❶ ◁ Stand opposite your partner in the formal stance position with your fists raised.

❷ ▷ Move into the back stance, with about 75 per cent of your weight on your rear leg, and prepare to block, using a downward circular motion, with the palm of your hand. Your fingers should be straight and locked together, with your thumb bent and locked inside the hand. Your left hand blocks your partner's right arm, striking his inner forearm. Have your right fist ready to make a counter-strike.

❸ △ Strike at your partner's floating rib with your right fist. Use hip momentum when delivering the strike.

△ Close-up of the strike into the neck area.

❹ ▷ Raise your right arm in a large circular motion to chop into your partner's neck, thus enabling you to eventually roll him down and apply a shoulder lock.

5 ◁ To develop this technique to a more advanced stage, apply a restraining technique by moving your left arm under your partner's right arm. *Note the posture and bent knees.*

6 ▷ Go with the restraint until you lock your partner well into your body. His right arm is now secured against the left side of your neck and both your hands are clasped above his right shoulder. Keep a low posture (horse stance) and keep your partner well secured and close to your body.

7 ◁ Bring your right arm up in front of your forehead, almost as if you are saluting.

8 ▷ Take hold of your partner's right wrist with your right hand and push his fingers outwards.

9 △ Continue to push his fingers and arm away from you. From this particular position you could then keep the momentum going and throw your partner, creating distance and giving you time to escape.

10 △ Alternatively, to restrain your partner, bring his right arm across his back in a figure-four arm lock.

ADVANCED
Technique | Passive defensive stance

The purpose of the passive defensive stance is to lull an attacker into a false sense of security. This is a combination of defusion skills using verbal communication and body language to throw the aggressor off guard. These are particularly advanced techniques requiring qualified supervision. The following demonstration is intended as a guide only.

❶ ◁ Step back with your left leg into the passive defensive stance. About 75 per cent of your weight should be on this leg. Bring your hands up level with your partner's eyes, palms facing forwards and fingers splayed. This depicts the body language of a submissive, calming nature. You are trying to communicate "I don't want any trouble".

❷ ▷ As your partner moves in and grabs your clothing, take hold of his right wrist with your left hand. Secure your partner's right hand with your left hand. Maintain a good, strong stance.

❸△ Using your right hand, flick at your partner's eyes to distract him.

△ This close-up shows the correct position, necessary for the securing hand grip.

❹ ▷ Bring your right arm up and over your partner's right arm. Keep his right wrist firmly secured with your left hand.

5 △Push through with your right arm under your partner's right elbow, in order to trap his arm.

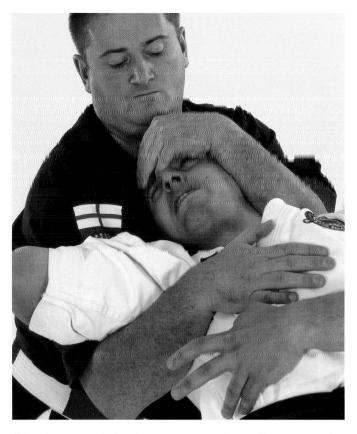

6 △ Place your right hand on your partner's chest, still maintaining the arm lock.

7 ◁ Bring your partner down to the floor by twisting his body in towards your chest. Ensure that your right arm is firmly placed on his chest, with the left hand restraining his forehead. It is important that you keep your partner as close to your body as possible in order to maintain control.

8 ◁ In a self-defence situation you may feel it necessary to strike in order to incapacitate an aggressor. One option is to strike with the knife edge of your hand into the groin area.

9 △ Alternatively, if you are an experienced practitioner and there is no danger from other quarters, you may wish to restrain an aggressor until assistance arrives.

Technique | Wrist defence

The following demonstrates one defence against a wrist attack, with the aim of countering the aggressor's initial attack and turning this to your advantage. Again, the combination of hard and soft is demonstrated by the use of wrist control (soft) and by striking techniques (hard).

❶△ Your partner moves in and grabs your wrists. Maintain your distance and move into a formal posture in preparation to defend.

❷△ With an open hand, push downwards and forwards.

❸△ Turn your wrist like a corkscrew against your partner's thumb, pushing your right hand straight down. Make sure to keep a deep, low stance for stability.

❹ △ Bring your hand right back, ready to strike with the back of your hand to the area of your partner's groin.

❺▷ Strike your partner's groin area with the back of your right hand.

6△ Take hold of your partner's elbow with your right hand.

7△ Your left hand begins to roll outwards from your partner's grip.

8△ Twist your left hand in an inwards and outwards circular action so that it rotates your wrist and is freed from the grip.

9△ While holding on to your partner's right arm with your right hand at the elbow joint, prepare for a left-hand palm heel strike. Still holding your partner's elbow joint, release your left hand in preparation to strike.

10△ Strike your partner in the face with the heel of your open hand.

11△ Overview of the technique showing your partner starting to move backwards. Dependent upon the force and angle of the strike, your partner, if an aggressor, would either fall to the floor or stagger backwards.

Technique | Elbow restraint

The following defence could be used against a variety of attacks, such as a push or a grab to the chest. Dependent upon the circumstances, you may prefer to restrain your opponent, rather than strike or throw. Restraining the arm, by applying pressure to the elbow, can be particularly effective, as demonstrated below.

1 △ Your partner moves in to push you in the chest by placing his hand on the region of your solar plexus. This could also be a grab at your clothing.

2 △ Immediately place your hand across your partner's right hand, pinning it against your body. Always practise using your right and left hands in a self-defence situation.

3 △ Place your hand firmly across your partner's hand to prevent him grabbing you while you begin to apply the elbow restraint.

4 △ Place your left hand behind your partner's elbow while maintaining your grip on his hand. Push in from his elbow towards the centre of your body to apply a wrist lock.

5 ▷ Continue pushing inwards and upwards. This will cause an aggressor extreme pain, as well as lifting him on to his toes and unbalancing him.

Technique | Defence from rear stranglehold

It is important to cover all eventualities and attacks from different positions. The following looks at one technique which can be applied against a rear stranglehold. The intention could be to pull you back, so the following demonstrates the use of the body position to minimize the attack in preparation to strike.

❶ ◁ Your partner grabs you around the throat, either to pull you back or to try to strangle you.

❷ ▷ Turn into a low horse stance position by jumping half a turn to your right. With your left hand open, defend your head area with a palm heel facing towards your partner. Close the fingers of your right hand to make a fist, in preparation to strike your partner.

❸ ◁ Strike your partner with a hammer fist to his floating rib.

Technique | Tactical search technique

The following arrest and restraint technique is used when you attempt to apprehend an aggressor who may be attacking you or another individual. This particular technique is mainly used by the armed forces and police, especially in riot situations. In view of its complexity, this technique requires qualified supervision and tuition.

1 △ As you come up behind the aggressor, grab the back of his clothing at the base of his neck, with your left hand. Keep your distance to prevent rear attack such as a kick.

2 △ You then bring your right hand across the aggressor's throat in order to prevent any further assault.

3 △ Place your left hand on the aggressor's forehead to secure a headlock. Note that the aggressor is being pulled backwards in order to upset his balance.

4 △ Now step back and go down on to your left knee, ensuring that the head lock is still securely in place. Your right leg should be jutting out with a 90-degree bend on your knee to ensure a good posture.

5 △ Bring your right leg around the aggressor's right arm and pull it back to secure a further restraint lock.

6 △ Kneel to secure the arm lock. Ensure that your body weight is leaning over the opponent for maximum control. Make the arm lock close to the body ensuring that the aggressor cannot manoeuvre his way out of the technique.

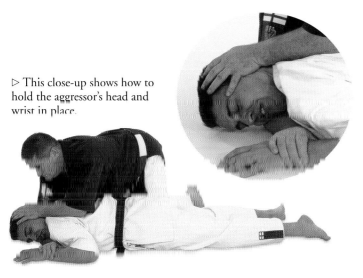

▷ This close-up shows how to hold the aggressor's head and wrist in place.

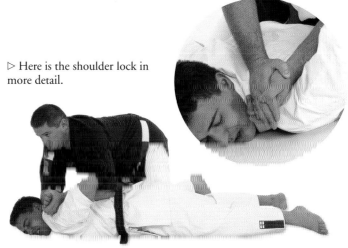

▷ Here is the shoulder lock in more detail.

7 △ Roll the aggressor around on to his front, keeping the head lock as secure as possible. Release your right hand and take hold of the aggressor's left wrist, with your left hand securely on top of his head in the ear and temple region. Lean across the back of the aggressor so that your body weight makes an effective restraint.

8 △ Maintain a secure arm lock and place your right hand across the back of the aggressor's neck. Start to manoeuvre your body upwards in preparation for the next part of the restraint.

△ This shows the exact hand and arm positions.

9 △ Bring your left knee across the upper part of the aggressor's body, maintaining the shoulder lock, and push his arm up his back, keeping your body weight slightly forward.

10 ▷ Lift the aggressor's arm up his back to secure the restraint.

11 △ Bring the aggressor's left arm across the front of your body, and to your right side, to effect a locking action.

12 △ At this point the aggressor is fully restrained and can be searched. A search could be carried out if, for example, you were the armed forces, police or security. Start in the area of his neck, working down his spine and into the rear of his waistband. Then search the inside and outside of his legs and groin and other areas of his body.

Technique | Knife defence

There are a variety of knife techniques practised in ju-jitsu. Unless extremely experienced and highly qualified, a dummy knife is always used for safety. Using a dummy knife assists the practitioner to get the feel of an aggressor who may use a weapon of any description. Such practice can enhance the reflexes in the event of a real knife threat.

ATTACK TO THE STOMACH — *Learning to develop body evasion skills against a weapon.*

1 △ An attacker draws his knife and threatens your stomach.

2 △ Breathe in and turn to your side, clasping the aggressor's knife hand close to the flat of your stomach.

3 △ Draw your elbow back in to pull the aggressor off balance and to keep him close in to you.

4 ◁ Strike to the aggressor's face, or any other part of his body that is accessible and vulnerable. This will disorientate the aggressor.

5 △ Now take a firm double-handed grip on the aggressor's knife hand and prepare to sweep through with your left leg.

6 △ As you sweep your left leg around, moving in towards the aggressor, keep the knife well away from your body. This is a flowing movement which prepares you for the take-down and restraint.

7 ▷ After the aggressor is on the floor, make sure that the knife is still well away from your body.

△ This is the same position from a different angle.

△ Close-up of the wrist restraint disarming the aggressor of the knife.

8 ▷ Apply a knee lock to the aggressor's elbow, maintaining the restraint until assistance arrives.

FACE SLASH — *Close range evasive tactics.*

1 △ An aggressor moves in with a knife attack to your face. Step back and prepare to use a double-handed knife-edge block to the aggressor's right arm.

2 △ A double block requires both hands simultaneously striking the aggressor's attacking arm, to ensure the knife does not make contact. The use of both hands reinforces the ability to defend more effectively.

3 △ Keeping the knife attack away from your body, move in sideways and strike with your elbow to the aggressor's floating rib or solar plexus, depending on which is more accessible.

4 △ Feed your right hand through in a snake-like movement, bringing your hand over the aggressor's right wrist to create an arm lock (key lock).

5 ◁ Continue the momentum, keeping the knife well away from your body, and take the aggressor down to the floor. Apply a finishing strike, if necessary.

REAR ATTACK – *Learning how to escape from a rear-arm lock.*

❶△ An aggressor moves in and grabs you in an arm lock from behind.

❷△ Step forwards and simultaneously grab the aggressor's wrist to pull him off balance.

❸ △ Strike with the knife edge of your left hand to the area of the aggressor's groin.

❹△ Following the groin strike, move under the aggressor's right arm in preparation to apply an arm lock. Keep both hands on the aggressor's right wrist to secure the restraint.

❺▷ Final technique demonstrating the application of a knee strike. In all cases, it is better to remain with a restraint, in view of the injuries which could be inflicted by using a "hard" strike.

Technique | Weapons

The following will give you an insight into some of the weapons (*kobojutsu*) and techniques used in ju-jitsu. Many of these weapons developed from practical farming tools used in everyday life many centuries ago. Qualified supervision and guidance must be sought when learning to use any weapons, and the following is for demonstration purposes only.

KAMMA – A kamma is a type of sickle used to cut moss, hay and corn. It was developed centuries ago on the Japanese island of Okinawa.

❶ △ This demonstrates the correct position in which to hold the *kamma*. Your body should be upright, your feet a shoulder-width apart and a *kamma* in each hand, in a crossed position, with the right hand uppermost.

❷ △ From here, move into a basic ready position by moving your right foot back into a long stance. Draw the right-hand *kamma* above your head, ready for a downwards strike, and hold the left-hand *kamma* in a forwards position as a defensive guard.

❸ △ From this position, step forwards with your right foot, bringing your right hand down in a striking movement. Draw the left-hand *kamma* back ready for a follow-up strike if necessary.

❹ ◁ Here, each *kamma* is being held in a blocking and striking position. The wooden part of the *kamma* could be used to deflect a strike, while being in the ready position for a follow-up strike.

❺ ▷ The *kamma* was traditionally used by peasants against aggressors. This stance would be used to assist the cutting-up motion of the *kamma* towards an opponent's groin or lower body.

SAI – The sai *was mainly used as a defensive weapon against a sword, staff, stick or empty hand. It was a popular weapon used on the island of Okinawa.*

2 ◁ Seen from the rear, the *sai* resting against the forearms and body are clearly visible.

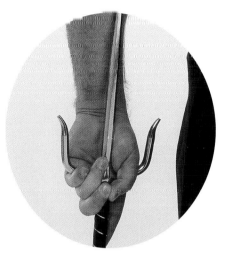

△ A close-up of the *sai* demonstrates the fingers and thumb positions.

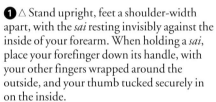

1 △ Stand upright, feet a shoulder-width apart, with the *sai* resting invisibly against the inside of your forearm. When holding a *sai*, place your forefinger down its handle, with your other fingers wrapped around the outside, and your thumb tucked securely in on the inside.

3 △ The *sai* being flicked inwards and outwards in a guard position, ready to guard and/or strike.

4 △ The left-hand *sai* being used in a blocking position, while the one in the right hand is ready to strike.

TONFA – The tonfa *in Japan comes from the island of Okinawa, although it is thought to have originated in China. This baton-like implement was adapted from an agricultural tool used for grinding coal, maize and corn. Today it is used as an effective defensive, blocking and striking weapon.*

❶ ◁ In the starting position, stand upright with your feet a shoulder-width apart, and with the *tonfa* held hidden behind your forearms.

△ A close-up view of the correct grip on the *tonfa*.

❷ ▷ Note how the fingers and thumb are securely wrapped along the top part of the *tonfa*, so that it can be used as a blocking device, as well as pivoting through the hand as a striking weapon.

❸ ◁ This illustrates one of the positions adopted when up against an armed opponent. The left-hand *tonfa* is aligned against the edge of the forearm, where it can block any incoming blow.

❹ ▷ The right-hand *tonfa* is held flexibly, so that it can be twirled in a circular action to strike an opponent across the head.

BO – The bo *is a 6ft (2m) pole made of red or white oak (red here), about 1½ in (3.5 cm) in diameter. Traditionally the* bo *developed from the staff (long pole) used by Buddhist priests.*

❶ ◁ This is the basic stance when using a *bo*, which should be held at the side of the body behind the right arm.

❷ ▷ Before striking with the *bo*, the practitioner steps back in a large circular motion.

TANTO-JUTSU – *The* tanto *was used specifically to attack at close quarters the weak points of an opponent's armour. It could easily be concealed and was particularly popular with both men and women as a form of defence, to attack vulnerable areas at close range.*

JO – *The* jo *is similar to the* bo, *but it is much shorter – about 4 ft (1.2 m). It is also lighter and usually smaller in diameter. It is held in a similar fashion to the* bo. *There is a famous story of the* jo *being used to defeat a 16th-century* samurai *warrior called Musashi Miyamoto.*

△ This classic guard stance is used to deliver an attack with this short-range weapon.

△ The *jo* practitioner is seen here having delivered a strike to an opponent's throat or solar plexus. Note the stance, with his legs crossed over and knees bent for stability.

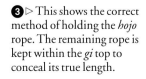

HOJO JUTSU – Hojo jutsu *is the traditional art of binding and restraining an aggressor on the battlefield. It is probably most commonly used today in security situations by the armed forces and military (it is a speciality of the Tokyo riot police). The purpose of the* hojo jutsu *techniques is to immobilize an opponent or aggressor until assistance arrives, or while they are being transported to a place of safety. The rope is traditionally 20 ft (6 m) long, which is twice the length of an adult martial arts belt* (obi). *It was traditionally worn around the waist and over the top of the armour. Today's martial arts practitioner would wear the* hojo jutsu *rope inside the jacket* (dogi).

❶ ◁ This picture portrays one of the *hojo jutsu* techniques to restrain an opponent. This is a specialized technique requiring considerable skill and special training.

❷ ▷ Here you can see that no knots are used – restraint is based on a series of loops and half hitches.

❸ ▷ This shows the correct method of holding the *hojo* rope. The remaining rope is kept within the *gi* top to conceal its true length.

JUDO

Judo, meaning "the gentle way", is regarded as a modern sport, deriving from ju-jitsu. The essence of judo is the skilful application of a combination of techniques, such as the power of resistance and effective timing. The main focus of judo, however, is the utilization of your opponent's body weight and strength against him or herself. There is some similarity in principle between judo and sumo wrestling, in that a small person can overcome a much larger opponent using skill, strategy and technique.

JUDO

history and philosophy

Professor Jiguro Kano, the founder of judo, graduated from the Imperial University of Tokyo, Japan, in 1881. He attended several ju-jitsu schools, seeking to develop a system of physical exercise. He adopted the best principles of each ju-jitsu system and called it judo, which, literally translated, means "gentle way". Kano's interpretation, however, was "maximum efficiency". He came to Europe in 1889 to spread the practice and philosophy of judo.

Kano envisaged judo as the development of a lifetime art, as opposed to a sport. Unusual for his time, he spoke perfect English and, breaking with Japanese tradition, his great respect for women prompted him to take on a female martial arts student, Sueko Ashiya. Criticisms were made that teaching women martial arts could lead to health problems because they had certain physical and other limitations that made them unsatisfactory students. Concerned with these comments, Kano undertook research into the impact that judo had on women, utilizing the knowledge of some of the leading medical experts of his day.

The research refuted his critics' claims concerning the negative impact of judo on women, and it was at about this time that Kano set up a *dojo* (training hall) for women in Koubun school, Tokyo. By 1935 judo was being successfully taught to women, especially in high school.

The first international judo tournament took place between Great Britain and France in 1947. Britain took the

Dismissing early doubts, judo was being taught to women by 1935.

title but, in 1951, the first European Championship was won by a French team. By 1956, judo was being taught in many Japanese schools. Unfortunately, Kano was not to witness any of this, since he died in1938, while at sea, returning from the Cairo International Olympic Conference. Some people claim that he was assassinated because of his actions and manifest sympathies towards the West.

It is worth bearing in mind that Kano did not create judo to be a public competition sport, and he felt strongly that it was a personal art to train the mind and body. He insisted that its mastery required an appreciation of the inherent philosophy that supports all aspects of judo. With this in mind, it is interesting to read the oath that all judo students at the *Kodukan dojo* (the name given by Kano to his *dojo*) must make on admission: "Once I have entered the *Kodukan*, I will not end my study without reasonable cause; I will not dishonour the *dojo*; unless I am given permission, I will not disclose the secrets that I have been taught; unless I am given permission, I will not teach judo; pupil first, teacher second, I will always follow the rules of the *dojo*."

Demonstrating the dynamic throws in judo.

Close quarter gripping in preparation to throw or defend.

Competition

Judo today is one of the most wide-spread martial arts in the world, with reputedly more than 8 million students. Practitioners are referred to as *judoka* and competitions (*shiai*) are conducted under the supervision of a referee and judge. Contests and training take place in the *judojo* (hall). Free-style combat in judo is known as *randori*; the submitting opponent is known as the *uke*; and the winning partner is referred to as the *tori* in judo.

More than just sport

Judo is not purely about physical skill. Its aim is to teach good attitude and behaviour and to instil a sense of decorum in its *judoka*: best summed up in two terms used to describe the mental attitude expected from a *judoka*: *hontai*, demonstrating the state of permanent alertness and *bonno*, demonstrating a disciplined mind, serene and calm, controlling the body and being able to react to any situation.

Judo is suitable for people of all ages and abilities and is one of the more popular martial arts.

"Judo is the means of understanding the way to make the most effective use of both physical and spiritual power and strength. By devoted practice and rigid discipline, in an effort to obtain perfection in attacking and defending, it refines the body and soul and helps instil the spiritual essence in judo into every part of one's very being. In this way, it is possible to perfect oneself and contribute something worthwhile to the world." JIGURO KANO

BENEFITS OF JUDO

Judo is suitable for people of all ages and abilities, and the benefits to be derived from it affect many aspects of your everyday life. These include:

- Health, fitness and stamina
- Confidence and well-being
- Self-defence skills
- Comradeship
- Flexibility and agility
- Awareness and assertiveness
- Strengthened limbs

Demonstrating the skill of break-falling.

It is very important that the training area is always kept clean and tidy. Ideally the floor should be swept before practice and usually the first student to arrive would undertake this responsibility. Any cause for concern, such as holes or chips in the floor area, must be noted and avoided. All practitioners must be aware of both emergency exits and emergency procedures e.g. local hospital number, emergency number and escape route. The first aid kit must always be available in the dojo.

clothing *and* equipment

A judo practitioner, a *judoka*, wears a *judogi*. This consists of a heavy cotton jacket and trousers made of strong material so that it can withstand the many grabs and tugs delivered in the judo "way of gentleness" (Jiguro Kano 1860–1938). The word judo is based on jikishin-ryu of ju-jitsu. Jiguro Kano wanted to turn ju-jitsu into a "martial sport" to train and educate young people. Kano said "the aim of Judo is to understand and demonstrate the living laws of movement".

The techniques which upset an opponent's balance and/or immobilize him or her is known as *kuzushi*. The main aim of judo is to neutralize an opponent as opposed to injure or kill. It is very much viewed as a self-defence system.

Judoka train with bare feet on the matted (*tatami*) area.

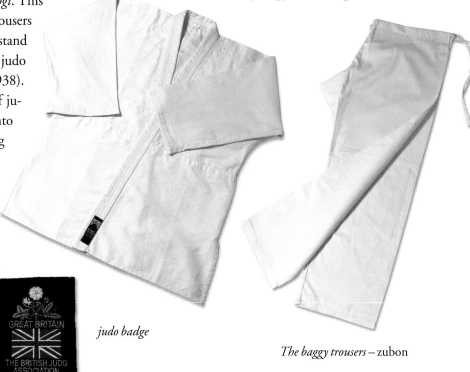

Wide fitting jacket – uwagi

judo badge

The baggy trousers – zubon

BELT GRADINGS

9th-*kyu*	Yellow
7th–8th-*kyu*	Orange
5th–6th-*kyu*	Green
3rd–4th-*kyu*	Blue
1st–2nd-*kyu*	Brown
1st–5th-*dan*	Black
6th–7th-*dan*	Red and white
8th–10th-*dan*	Red

All beginners wear a white belt and there is a different belt sequence for junior practitioners.

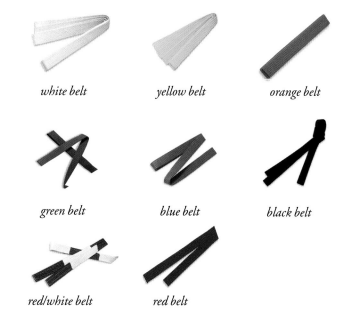

white belt   *yellow belt*   *orange belt*

green belt   *blue belt*   *black belt*

red/white belt   *red belt*

Etiquette

Etiquette and discipline are of the utmost importance in judo, not only to maintain respect and courtesy for the art and your opponent, but also to ensure safety. All practitioners must look after their personal appearance – especially their nails, which can scratch if they are too long or ragged.

❶ ↘ Stand upright and relaxed, with your eyes looking forwards and your feet a shoulder-width apart.

❷ ▷ Perform the bow by inclining your body by about 30 degrees. Let your eyes follow the bow to the floor, since this is given as a sign of respect to the art, the training environment and your fellow practitioners.

❸ ▷ When practising or in competition with a partner, the same bow is performed. It is important to allow adequate space between yourself and your partner to avoid bumping heads! Ideally, you need to be at approximately one and a half arms distance, as this maintains a safe personal boundary. In competition, you take one step back and then bow to your partner.

Exercise | Warm-up

The idea behind this exercise routine is to loosen the whole of your body, making your muscles and joints as flexible as possible, in order to prevent injuries during training. What is unique to judo is the emphasis on preparing the body for grappling and throwing moves. A general warm-up must be carried out first, in preparation for the actual techniques.

WARM-UP 1 – *Sit-ups help to develop stomach muscles and stamina. Be careful to build this exercise up gradually to avoid injury.*

◁ Lie flat on the floor. Bend your knees at approximately 90 degrees, never straight, with your partner holding your ankles. Place your hands at the sides of your head. The tips of your fingers should be in the region of your temples. Keep your elbows tucked in and raise your body about 45 degrees from the floor as you exhale. Then lower yourself down as you inhale. Repeat this exercise several times.

WARM-UP 2 – *The star jump assists in the overall body warm-up process and builds stamina.*

❶ ◁ For the star jump, stand in a relaxed, natural position, feet a shoulder-width apart, and hands at your sides.

❷ ▷ Jump into an X position – legs spread and arms raised – and then back into the standing position. Repeat this about ten times.

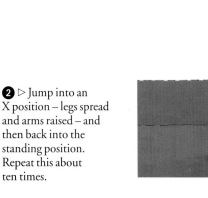

WARM-UP 3 – *Press-ups (push-ups) assist in developing the upper part of the body. Take your time and build up gradually and carefully.*

◁ Lie face down on the floor, with your legs slightly apart. Make sure you are on the balls of your feet and place your hands approximately in line with your shoulders. Slowly inhale as you raise your body upwards. Keep your body level and arms straight. Gently lower yourself, just touching the floor, but do not take the weight off your arms. Build up to sets of 10 if possible.

WARM-UP 4 – *Leg stretches, such as this inner-thigh stretch, are important as part of your preparation for judo practice*

◁ Sit on the floor with legs spread as far as possible. Lower your upper body as far as you comfortably can, towards your left knee. Keep your leg straight and aim to go a little further down each time you practise. Don't worry if you cannot manage this in the early stages: it takes time to become supple. Repeat 10 times to the left side and then the right side, holding for approximately 10 seconds.

WARM-UP 5 (*UCHI-KOME*) – *An important part of the warm-up routine is preparation for throwing.*

❶△ Face your partner and take hold of his right sleeve with your left hand. Your partner takes hold of your left lapel with his right hand. *Note: this technique is also performed to the opposite side e.g. left and right grabs.*

❷△ As you move, step through with your right foot and bring your right arm under your partner's left arm.

❸△ Rotate your body around until your back makes contact with your partner's front and your feet are in-between your partner's, with you legs slightly bent. Push your right hip back towards your partner and gently pull him forwards and downwards over your right shoulder. Remember, this is only an exercise, so don't carry the throw through. Return to the start position and repeat the exercise several times.

Technique | Basic throws

Throwing techniques form the basis of judo, aiming to disrupt the partner's point of balance, and therefore do not rely on strength, but on skill and good timing. Professional supervision is vitally important when practising all throws. The following techniques are only a guide to some of those used and are performed from both right and left grabs.

BODY DROP (*TIA-OTOSHI*) – *Disrupting the partner's point of balance in preparation to throw.*

❶ △ Stand facing your partner. Grab your partner's lapel with your right hand and her sleeve with your left hand. Your partner also takes hold of your lapel with her right hand and your left arm with her left hand.

❷ △ Step forwards with your right leg, turning your right shoulder in towards your partner. Keep an upright posture and maintian a secure grip of your partner's clothing in preparation for the throwing technique.

❸ △ Lower your stance to maintain good posture and balance, and use your body momentum to throw your partner.

HOOKING TECHNIQUE (*KO-UCHI GARI*) – *A smaller person can overcome a larger person.*

SWEEPING TECHNIQUE (*ASHI WAZA*)

❶ △ Your left arm is grabbed, above the elbow, by your partner. Move in close.

❷ △ Hook the inside of his right leg, and use your momentum to throw your partner backwards and downwards.

❸ ◁ Project your body forwards and throw him to the floor.

△ A popular technique in judo is the "sweep". The aim is to catch your partner's lower leg/foot with a scooping action as they move forwards, using the inside of your foot in an outwards and inwards motion. At the same time, grab your partner's clothing. Both partners must be well versed in break-falling and beginners must have qualified supervision.

Following a take down to the floor, a variety of restraints can be applied. When correctly performed, a partner can be kept restrained for some time. In competition, the partner has to be held for 25 seconds to qualify for any point(s). The following techniques would be applied to gain points if a throw has not been won.

△ After throwing your partner, pin her down by lying across her chest. Your right arm should be positioned around her right leg and your left arm around the back of her neck. Take hold of your partner's clothing where it is accessible. Spread your legs well apart to give good balance and to increase the pressure on your partner's body.

❶ ▷ If you are being attacked while sitting on the floor, control your partner with your legs and secure her head with your arms. Now turn her on to her back. Move through with your left arm in preparation for securing your partner and turning her towards the floor.

❷ ▽ Once you have turned your partner towards the floor, secure her by applying an upper body hold.

CAUTION

It is important to ensure that your partner's windpipe is not smothered by your restraint, so that they can breathe freely and advise you of any possible discomfort. This is particularly important in training where a technique is being demonstrated by an adult against a junior. Some techniques are not allowed to be practised on young people under the age of 16, particularly choking techniques.

Technique | Defence tactics

There are a variety of self-defence moves in judo which equip a student to deal with attacks from different angles. The following demonstrates a defensive move from a rear attack, using the opponent's body weight to their disadvantage. In judo, you learn to overcome your opponent's attack by displacing their centre of gravity.

SELF-DEFENCE 1

1 ◁ An aggressor grabs you around the neck from the rear, with his right arm placed across your throat.

2 ◁ Take hold of the aggressor's right sleeve and push your hips back into his body. At the same time, pull his right arm over your shoulder in a forward and downward action. Bend your legs and rotate your body so that you can throw your partner.

◁ This side view shows the same movement, and you can clearly see how projecting your hips backwards unbalances the aggressor. This demonstrates how to move into the aggressor's centre of gravity to break their point of balance. It also reveals how a smaller individual can overcome a larger person.

3 △ Keep the momentum going so that your opponent is thrown over your shoulder and on to the floor. The force of the throw should incapacitate him, giving you time to get to a safe place.

1 △ An aggressor is coming at you from the front and grabs the clothing on either side of your neck.

2 △ Place your hand under your partner's chin. Step forwards and sweep away the legs.

3 △ Maintain the pressure under his chin in order to break his balance.

4 △ Keep the momentum going and throw the aggressor to the floor.

▷ This side view of step 4 shows the hand grip in more detail.

Technique | Choke and strangle

This section demonstrates a variety of choke and strangle techniques. A choke is defined as putting pressure against the windpipe; a strangle is pressure against the blood supply, such as the jugular vein. These are highly-skilled techniques and the intention is to learn these as a means of developing advanced skills only.

CAUTION

These techniques are advanced moves developed for the purpose of restraining in a self-defence situation. They are very specialized and must be practised under strict supervision. Young people under 16 years old, in particular, must not practise certain moves, or have such techniques applied to them.

HADAKA-JIME
▽ The *hadaka-jime* is a choke technique in which the forearm is locked against the windpipe. It is important to keep your body close with feet astride to maintain control.

△ Place your forearm against your partner's windpipe and pull him towards you, forcing the head forward. Keep your hands well clasped together and secure your head close to your partner's. Any gaps will allow your partner to escape.

OKURI-ERI-JIME
▽ In this basic strangle technique (*okuri-eri-jime*), pressure is applied to the side of the neck, cutting the blood supply, as opposed to the air supply.

ADVANCED
Technique | Leg and arm locks

Here *juji-gatame* (straight-arm lock) and *ude-garame* (bent-arm lock) are demonstrated. *Juji-garame* is a complex groundwork technique which involves using both your arms and legs. The pressure that is applied by this technique restricts your opponent's ability to break free even when the arms and legs have limited movement.

JUJI GATAME
▷ By pinning the opponent in this position, their body is immobilized by the straight arm lock. Pull the arm across your body and lift your hips in order to apply pressure to the extended straight arm.

UDE-GARAME
▽ Take a figure 4 position with your arms and bend your opponent's arms upwards by pressing downwards on their wrist.

▷ There are several variations of this technique, namely a straight-arm lock (*juji-gatame*) and a bent-arm lock (*ude-garame*). *Ude-garame* is shown demonstrating the bent-arm lock as part of a floor restraining technique. *Note: you should be lying across your opponent with your legs splayed, to maintain body pressure.*

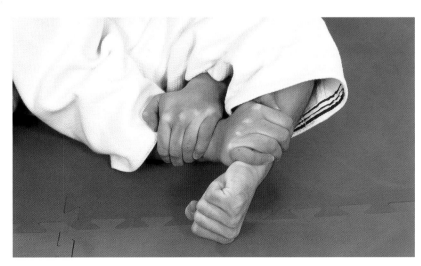

143

TECHNIQUE JUDO

K U N G   F U

Kung fu, meaning "sustained effort or skill" incorporates hundreds of styles such as wing chun and tai chi. However, there are common traits which complement the overall picture within kung fu. All disciplines start with basic stances and motions which act as a platform from which a student may learn and study different styles and forms. As skill levels rise, these forms progress into higher levels of difficulty, allowing the student to gain fluidity and dexterity before competitive training.

WING CHUN

history *and* philosophy

Wing chun kuen kung fu is just one of many styles of martial arts, whose origins are to be found in Southern China and, compared with other martial arts, it is a relative newcomer. The term wing chun is attributed to a woman called Yim Wing Chun, who was the protégé of a Buddhist nun called Ng Mui. Wing chun is known as a "soft" style, but is in fact a blend of both "hard" and "soft" techniques. With reference to the hard concept, in simple terms this means meeting force with force, whereas the soft term refers to more evasive manoeuvres and techniques.

Roughly translated, wing chun means "beautiful spring-time" and kuen means "fist" or "fist fighting style". However, many people refer to the style as being "wing chun". This blending of hard and soft is due to the fact that it was developed by a woman and refined mainly by men. It is also said that Ng Mui once observed a battle between a snake and a crane. From her observations sprang ideas on how to develop this art. Mimicking animal movements is particularly common in Chinese martial arts.

There are many varied accounts of the history of wing chun in relation to names, dates and places. The following attempts to give one account of the history of its origin.

*The late Grand Master of wing chun kung fu, Yip Mun, uses the wooden dummy apparatus (*mook yan jong*), in order to condition both body and mind, while also improving his kung fu techniques.*

Shaolin monks demonstrate breaking techniques.

During the reign of Emperor K'anghsi of the Ching Dynasty (1662-1722), the Shaolin monastery Siu Lam of Mt Sung, in the Honan province, had become very powerful through kung fu training. The Manchurian government, fearing an uprising, sent troops to destroy Siu Lam. However, the fate of the monastery was settled internally, with traitorous monks setting it alight. Only a handful of monks and disciples managed to escape the onslaught of the Manchurian army. Among these were Abbot Chi Shin, Abbot Pak Mei, Master Fung To Tak, Master Miu Him and Abbess Ng Mui. Ng Mui was a master of Siu Lam kung fu and and became the creator of the wing chun system.

Ng Mui's ideas of close-quarter combat were totally different from the Siu Lam system of that time. She discarded many of the old traditions, which often required years of dedicated practice at each stage, and started to develop a system based on the principle of winning at all costs, by using speed and subtlety to overcome an opponent's natural

advantages. Her system, as yet unnamed, therefore had less stress on muscular strength (*lik*), bone conditioning or muscular flexibility. The emphasis lay in sudden contraction and relaxation (*ging*) causing the practitioner to explode into

A stretching exercise typical of Southern Chinese martial arts.

The Zen-like appearance of the Shaolin temple evoked by nature – shaolin means small forest.

action, using natural weapons such as finger jabs to the eyes, elbow strikes to the face and the powerful use of knees and feet to an opponent's lower body.

Ng Mui later met and befriended a young, intelligent and beautiful woman named Yim Wing Chun, who was just fifteen years of age. Little is known of Yim's childhood, other than that her mother died when she was in her teens and her father, Yim Yee, was falsely accused of a crime. To avoid possible imprisonment, father and daughter moved to Mt Tai Leung, along the border of Hunan and Szechuan provinces. Here Yim soon attracted the attentions of a local

BONG SAU

One of the important techniques taught in wing chun is *bong sau* (meaning "wing arm"). It is taught to beginners as a basic cover against an attack, and is particularly useful to their understanding of the style. The technique is designed to protect a wide area of your body, to yield under extreme pressure yet never allowing your arm to become trapped. It can change easily into a palm-up block and allow you to slip your hand free. The rear protective guard hand (*wu sau*) can grab and deflect the incoming strike and allow the bong to become an effective throat-cutting technique.

This *bong sau* movement demonstrates just how flexible wing chun can be. It also illustrates that if a single technique can be used in many situations, why then learn several different moves for several different situations? This reinforces the simplicity of the system.

landowner, Wong. He attempted to bully her into marriage and even tried to rape her. It was at the Temple on Mount Tai Leung, where Ng Mui had taken refuge, that the two women met and befriended each other.

To help protect Yim Wing Chun, Ng Mui took her into the mountains and taught her the techniques of her new fighting system, in an effort to teach her how to protect herself. Under Ng Mui's direction, Yim studied kung fu religiously, and mastered the style. Naturally, Yim Wing Chun subsequently returned to her village and defeated the bully Wong, and it is believed that Ng Mui named her new style wing chun kuen, after her protégée.

Wing chun is centred on the Taoist principle of "take the middle road". In essence, this says that you should not go to extremes, and that success is based on balance. If you are on the middle road you can see both the left and right paths, but if you venture too far to one side you may lose sight of the other. This can also be interpreted as the concept of the hard and soft principles – or *yin* and *yang*. *Yin* (the feminine side) focuses on diverting the flow of energy; *yang* (the masculine side) seeks to resist any opposing energy flow. *Yang* is primarily seen in the explosive quality of the striking moves.

Subsequent generations of wing chun practitioners have refined the system further, but always keeping to the simple, almost scientific, principles of the art: the centre-line theory (protecting and striking at the major pressure points); economy of motion (keeping every movement as simple as possible); and the self-explanatory principle of combined or simultaneous defence and attack.

A Shaolin monk demonstrates the flexibility that can be achieved from practising this art.

The centre-line theory is viewed as being the most definitive part of the wing chun system, since there are many attacking strikes that seek to obscure the vision of an aggressor. The centre-line is also defensive, since your own vulnerable points are protected by the counter-attacks. The practitioner is not regarded as an aggressor in a martial arts situation, because wing chun is an art of self-defence. However, if you are fighting multiple assailants, the situation may dictate the need to attack aggressively. In this type of situation, wing chun practitioners find the use of finger strikes, elbows and knee kicks to be of great value. Even the most skilled wing chun practitioner can fight only one person at a time, so the need to strike and escape is the main objective.

"Sticky hands"

One of the most important techniques in wing chun is "sticky hands" (*chi sau*). Since wing chun is a close-quarter system, it is potentially dangerous for the practitioners themselves, who are at risk of being hit, grabbed or kicked. This realization has led to a particular training method called *sheung chi sau* ("double sticky hands").

To the uninitiated, this technique is best described as a hurt boxer trying to "spoil" his opponent's moves by clinging to his arms. The aim is to prevent an opponent striking freely, giving the wing chun practitioner the opportunity to control, trap and break free to strike. The real skill lies in both parties wanting to achieve the same goal, and this has led to exceptional techniques, in which either one or both parties can train blindfolded. A skilful practitioner can eventually predict and nullify the danger.

The main areas that "sticky hands" seeks to develop fall into the categories of sensitivity, power and general fitness. Sensitivity covers such aspects as the centre-line concept, reaction to direction change, striking when the hand is freed, going with the power and not resisting force, continuous techniques (fluidity), and balance in the vertical and horizontal planes. Power involves guiding power, aggressive and explosive power, and power control and balancing-power techniques.

BENEFITS OF WING CHUN

The benefits derived from learning wing chun affect many aspects of your everyday life. These include:

- Physical and emotional control
- Confidence and well-being
- Assertiveness and reflexes
- Health improvement through physical exercise, breathing and body movement
- Comradeship
- Stress reduction
- Good posture and stability
- Mobility and flexibility

clothing *and* equipment

Practitioners of wing chun usually wear casual, clean clothing consisting of a comfortable top and trousers. Soft footwear such as slippers are worn on the feet, along with protective equipment when it is necessary, such as gum shields. There is no official grading system in wing chun, although different organizations have now developed their own systems. The sash is an integral part of clothing yet does not depict any grade. A variety of weapons is used such as butterfly knives and the 6½ point pole. The wooden dummy (*mook yan jong*) is one of the main pieces of equipment used for training in wing chun.

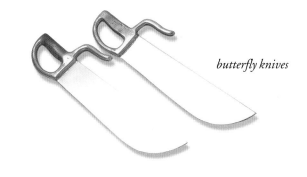

butterfly knives

A smartly dressed wing chun practitioner.

*The wooden dummy (*mook yan jong*) is an impressive piece of equipment and is unique to wing chun. It is designed as a replica of the human body, in terms of the position of the torso, hands and legs, and practitioners use it to develop their blocking and striking techniques.*

Etiquette

Etiquette is used as a sign of respect to the art, instructor, fellow practitioners and training area. As well as a sign of respect, the etiquette is used as a form of welcoming. The practitioner can smile when performing this ritual, as a warm friendly greeting, with no aggression intended.

SALUTATION 1

1 ◁ Stand in a relaxed position with your feet together and hands at the sides of your body. This is a formal manner of displaying etiquette in wing chun.

This etiquette is similar to the one may used in the Chinese New Year, which commences each February, and is part of a long tradition. As a part of this tradition the fist would be fully covered as a symbol of peace.

SALUTATION 2 – *There is an alternative formality, which is characterized by a particularly friendly facial expression.*

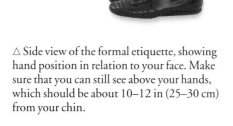

2 △ Make a fist with your right hand and nestle it into the palm of your left hand in front of your face, approximately at chin level. Keep the fingers of your left hand pointing upwards. This shows a more informal gesture.

△ Side view of the formal etiquette, showing hand position in relation to your face. Make sure that you can still see above your hands, which should be about 10–12 in (25–30 cm) from your chin.

△ Stand as you would for the formal *rei* above, but note that the fingers of your left hand curl over the fist, partially hiding it from view. Your facial expression should be receptive and pleasant – almost like saying "hello".

Exercise | Warm-up

The following is a selection of warm-up exercises found in wing chun. In view of the close-range techniques and circular action required in certain moves, emphasis is placed on forearm power to improve strength and suppleness. Strong wrists and forearms protect the practitioner from injury upon striking and help transmit the force more effectively.

WARM-UP 1 – *This exercise is designed to make your wrists supple and increase their flexibility.*

1 ◁ Kneel on the floor, facing forwards. Place both hands on the floor in front of you with the fingers facing backwards, towards your knees. Your back should be slightly arched. Keep looking forwards. *Note: it is the body weight on your wrists that enhances the effect of this exercise, but be careful to increase pressure gently, with practice, over a period of time.*

2 ◁ Remain in the kneeling position and turn your right hand inwards, palm uppermost, and fingers facing towards your left arm. Gently apply pressure on the wrist, increasing the weight with practice, over a period of time. Hold for approximately 30 seconds and repeat the exercise with your left hand. Repeat 2 or 3 times.

WARM-UP 2 – *The following is a series of actions extracted from the wing chun first form* sui nim tao *designed to increase flexibility of the wrists. Perform all movements with the right hand first. This* heun sau *sequence translates as "circling hand" and is of fundamental importance to wing chun.*

❶ △ Start in a palm up position with feet a shoulder-width apart. Keep your withdrawn arm high at chest level and place your right hand, palm uppermost, in front of you. Slightly bend your elbow. Position your left fist just above your left hip. Your elbow needs to be positioned about 5 in (13 cm) from your chest. Rotate your outstretched hand in an inwards, circular motion, starting and finishing with the palm in the upwards position. Repeat 3 or 4 times and change to the left hand.

❷ △ Twist your outstretched hand inwards, with your fingers facing back towards your body. Make sure your thumb is tucked in. Your fingers need to be close together to maximize the benefit of this exercise. Hold for 10–20 seconds. From step 1 bring your fingers up and back towards the body.

❸ △ Twist your hand with an inward-turning circular action. This technique is called *fook sau* (bridge on arm). Hold for 10–20 seconds.

❹ △ Continue the *fook sau* by pushing the tips of your fingers downwards, forming part of the circular action.

❺ △ Complete the circle so the hand finishes, fingers facing upwards, with the wrist pushing in a short and powerful descent. This technique is called *jum sau*. Bring the palm back closer to the body and repeat steps 3, 4 and 5 again. Repeat as often as required.

Technique | *Kau sau*

Kau sau (circling hand or arm movement) is a popular exercise in wing chun. It is often used in demonstrations to give a "feel" for the art. It is an exercise which requires the assistance of a partner in order to develop their wing chun skills. It also seeks to develop a practitioner's evasive and striking skills.

❶ ◁ The partners stand opposite each other in the ready position – both adopt frontal guard positions. Only the left practitioner is demonstrating wing chun.

❷ ▷ Your partner strikes at your face with his right fist. Step back and block with your right inner arm. This technique is called *gaan sau* or "splitting block".

❸ △ Circle your partner's right wrist with your defending hand and counter-attack by stepping through and striking with your left fist to your partner's short ribs.

❹ ▷ Bring the low punch up and support the elbow (*tok sau*). Use both arms to pull your partner on to a low front kick. In this sequence the opponent's forwards momentum is used to your advantage.

Technique | *Chi sau*

Chi sau ("sticky hands") is one of the most famous techniques practised in wing chun. The term "sticky hands" is used to describe the continuous contact made between the two practitioners. In order to develop this technique you need to attend regular classes under professional supervision. The following steps give an insight only into the style.

❶ ▷ Stand in a relaxed fashion, opposite your partner, with your feet a shoulder-width apart and your arms in contact with your partner's forearms. Look forwards. Gently rotate your arms.

❷ ▷ Keep rotating your arms upwards and downwards, maintaining contact with your partner's forearms and wrists. You should sense a flow of energy throughout this contact.

❸ △ The practitioner on the left senses an overlap in the arms and penetrates the centre, moving from the outside left of his partner, to the outside right. He pushes through and pulls the head forwards from the back of the neck (*man geng sau*).

❹ ▷ The practitioner then follows up with an elbow strike to the face (*cup jarn*). *Note that the opponent's arms are temporarily trapped.*

Technique | Children's practice

When children practise any of the martial arts, it is very important that they receive strict and professional supervision. It is also important that they keep a good distance away from each other to prevent accidental injuries. All exercise and practice must be appropriate to the age of the child and their stage of physical and mental development.

❶ ◁ When children are practising techniques, they should stand far enough apart so that any strikes miss by between 5–8 in (13–20 cm). This is especially important when striking towards the face area.

❷ ▷ Your partner uses a left fist strike towards your face. Notice, however, that the strike finishes well short of the face.

❸ △ Defend against the attack by bringing your right arm upwards in a circular motion. The emphasis on turning the body, to avoid or redirect force, makes wing chun ideal for young people, as there is less chance of a direct strike making contact.

❹ ▷ Follow through with a right-hand striking technique to the bridge of your partner's nose. Make sure you are holding your partner's left wrist with your left hand. In this technique the practitioner has placed his fist on his partner's nose to demonstrate the striking area. When practising with movement, he would keep at a safe distance, as recommended.

Technique | *Taan sau*

Taan sau is a very typical wing chun kuen blocking move and is practised by all ages. It develops the ability, not to intercept a strike with counter-strike, but to place a cover in the way and attempt to turn. This is why blocking in wing chun kuen is often termed "bridging arms", meaning it is used to find the arm.

1 ◁ Stand opposite your partner with your feet a shoulder width apart and both fists at the sides of your body. Bend your knees slightly and look towards your partner. This closes the inner area of the legs and ensures the groin and knees are better protected when turning. This is the basic ready position for *taan sau*, and it is important to note how close you stand to your partner.

2 ▷ Your partner uses a right fist strike towards your face, ensuring a safe distance to avoid physical contact. The closeness of the strike will be determined by experience. Maintain your posture and focus as you prepare to defend.

3 ◁ Defend against this strike by using a forward and upward open-hand block with your left hand. Keep your right hand in an open-guard position, ready to push your partner away, or prepare to either block or strike. Make sure to push the attack away by intercepting the punch as soon as possible.

4 ▷ Counter-attack by delivering a right-hand fist strike to the solar plexus. Ensure that your technique is correctly focused to avoid any injury to your partner. In this photograph the fist has made contact to demonstrate the correct target position. When actually using speed and force, it is important to maintain your focus, depending on the level of your ability.

Technique | *Rolling arm – Lok sau*

Wing chun is particularly useful for women. The fact that the founder was a woman is significant, since the close-range techniques used do not necessarily require strength or force. What is required is skill, timing and anticipation to know when a vulnerable area is available to strike. The following guide for beginners requires qualified supervision.

2 △ Place your right hand on your partner's right arm ready to twist and turn (*laap sau* means deflecting arm).

1 △ Face your partner with your feet a shoulder-width apart, keep your back straight and look forwards. Your hands should be forward and forearms in contact with your partner. This is the ready position for *lok sau* practice.

3 △ Maintain a rolling action that delivers a certain amount of pressure on your partner.

WING CHUN   TECHNIQUE

4 ◁ The technique has now completely reversed from the beginning.

5 △ As in step 2, move on to perform the same technique, taking you back to step 1. You will find the technique alternating between you and your partner.

6 △ You now change sides to perform an alternative to continuing to roll back and forth with your arms. As you feel your partners desire to deflect your arm, take hold of their arm and deliver a right punch. Your partner, feeling the grab, responds by blocking the incoming strike through performing a left *bong sau*.

7 ▷ The sequence now follows through as in steps 1–4. Whenever there is an attempt to deflect the strike, the other side has a chance to grab and change sides. This sequence develops good reaction to grabs, punches and change of direction. This technique can be developed to an extremely high speed with the correct supervision and lots of practice.

Technique | *Mook yan jong*

Wooden dummy practice (*mook yan jong*) is used to develop various blocks and strikes. It represents the human body and was invented by Ng Mui as she stood by a well collecting water. It is a unique piece of equipment found only in the art of wing chun and it plays an integral part in a practitioner's development of the techniques.

◁ Demonstrates a low kick used to break an opponent's stance.

▽ Demonstrates a sweep kick and counter-strike.

◁ Demonstrates a double-palm push known as *po pai jeung*.

▷ A complex movement called *gaan sau*, meaning "splitting block".

Many of the weapons in wing chun have developed from everyday practical tools used in farming, such as rice flails, or boating, such as poles and staffs. These are common to nearly all Chinese martial arts. Staffs were used to carry water to and from wells and thus techniques for self-defence developed from familiar objects to hand.

▷ The first weapon to be demonstrated is the *luk dim boon kwun*, an 8 ft (2.5 m) length of sturdy, tapering wood, known as the 6½ point pole. This refers to the six main movements where the pole is used to block and strike, as well as small half movements. It is tapered at one end to prevent it becoming excessively heavy and allow the tip to be moved faster. The pole derives from the similar object that the boat people used to push their boats away from the bank. It was also used for carrying water, with a container at either end.

◁ Using the hilt of the butterfly knives to trap and control a spear or pole attack.

△ The butterfly knives being used for "trapping the spear".

△ A deflective movement known as *laap do*.

MOK-GAR

history *and* philosophy

Shaolin mok-gar kuen is one of the original family disciplines of kung fu, from Southern China, and is well-known for its kicking techniques. Practitioners are not restricted just to kicking, however, since the use of a full range of weapons is also part of the system. The resulting flexibility of attack and defence epitomizes the original concept of Chinese martial arts: to express yourself fully in the attempt to triumph in combat. When engaging in combat, the objective is to win, so practitioners believe that to place any restrictions on one particular movement would be to put themselves at a disadvantage.

Shaolin mok-gar kuen, so legend has it, was originally developed by a midget called Mok-Da-Si, in the Shaolin monastery in Southern China. He taught this style, known then as shaolin chuen, to his family in the Tong-Kwun district of Kwong-Tong province, and the name was retained until the third generation, when it was renamed mok-gar (after Mok's family).

The style has passed virtually unchanged through many generations, and is still faithfully taught today, according to its original concept. Indeed, it shares the same good reputation with four other contemporary Southern Chinese family styles: hung-gar, choi-gar, lee-gar and lau-gar. Each family

The spirit of kung fu is often reflected within the face and poise of Asian temple guardians.

The elegant roof of a Shaolin temple with ornate wood carvings.

The training stumps upon which Shaolin monks would stand to improve their skills of balance and one-on-one harmony.

became well-known for its specific strength within the style. The Chinese have a traditional saying, which when translated, calls to mind the strong points of these styles: "Hung's fists, mok's kicks and lee's staff."

Mok-gar kuen practice traditionally involves the use of two wooden dummies. One is called *mook-yan-jong*, with projections which resemble arms, and is used for blocking and countering. The other is called *darn gee* and is particular to mok-gar. The *darn gee* consists of a hollow bamboo post 13 ft (4 m) high and 4 in (10 cm) in diameter, which is set into the ground by about 3 ft (1 m). It is filled with washers (originally coins) and is used to practise all of the attacks necessary for a student to learn. This training is excellent for building physical power and developing effective punches and kicks. This is important in mok-gar, since every student has to pass through a stage where he or she develops a considerable amount of power before progressing.

One of the unique training drills found in mok-gar kuen is that of the *darn gee* kicking technique. In kung fu, each school has its own method of teaching the kicks using various mechanical facilities. Irrespective of the method, the aim is the same: to increase the freedom of leg movements, enhance speed, improve accuracy, and to develop and harden the soles of the feet.

During the course of training, the *darn gee* helps practitioners to improve their stamina, hardness, speed, accuracy

Well-known for its kicking techniques, mok-gar kuen kung fu also teaches how to withstand being kicked. Here a Shaolin monk is totally open to a vicious groin kick.

and strength in kicking techniques. This unique training drill is a stage that all mok-gar practitioners must experience if they wish to develop a high standard within this style. The 108 movements that are the basis of the mok-gar style can be used in many ways, from just a single punch, which may be all that is needed to win a fight, to multiple jumping kicks.

When experienced, students progress to learning a soft form of kung fu, called tai chi. Sifu Chan, who came to England to develop the system which incorporated the use of weapons, teaches the wu style tai chi, based on the Taoist symbol of yin and yang (soft and hard). Tai chi teaches you to be aware of, and to react to, any form of attack, and to be ever-changing and formless. To learn and combine these two systems of kung fu is not an easy task, but once acquired, the knowledge and experience can prove invaluable.

Madame Mok Kwei Lan

Madame Mok Kwei Lan, known as the Tigress, was only a teenager when she started giving kung fu instruction some sixty years ago. Madame Mok was a native of Kao Yao, a small town near Canton. As a child, she was taught the family art of mok-gar kung fu – known as "Snapping the Iris" – by her uncle. In the face of strong disapproval – women were not encouraged to learn martial arts – she continued to study secretly with her uncle, by whom she was eventually adopted, with her parents' approval. She eventually married her uncle's friend, Wong Fei Hung, whom she assisted by

looking after his gymnasium, giving kung fu instruction and practising as a trained osteopath.

There are many stories regarding Madame Mok, as the Tigress, being challenged to fight. One particular incident occurred after she had moved to Hong Kong and was living in the Wanchai district. Once, when buying food in the marketplace, Madame Mok saw four men bullying a fishmonger. As she intervened to help him, the four men turned on her and attacked her with poles. She then proceeded to take away all of the men's weapons and knocked the aggressors down one by one. The four attackers ran away in great pain, as the onlookers clapped with delight. Stories regarding this incident spread far and wide, enhancing her already formidable reputation.

BENEFITS OF MOK-GAR KUEN

The benefits derived from learning mok-gar kuen affect many aspects of your everyday life. These include:

- **Flexibility and durability**
- **Confidence and assertiveness**
- **Stamina and fitness**
- **Health and well-being**
- **Comradeship**
- **Stress reduction**

The ability to defend oneself against an armed attacker is the mark of a competent and assured mok-gar kuen practitioner.

Demonstrating a technique to a group of students.

clothing *and* equipment

In general, practitioners of mok-gar wear a white T-shirt, which may or may not depict black writing showing the name of the art and training area, together with black trousers. Instructors may wear red trousers. It is also permissible for instructors to wear a white mandarin jacket. Trainers (sneakers) or bare feet are permissible during the practice of mok-gar. Weapons in mok gar include the three-sectional staff, spear, staff, split staff, *siu so gee*, *tee-chec*, *dip do* (butterfly knives), *guay*, pegs, broad sword, tai chi sword, three-section and nine-section steel whip.

SASH GRADING

Instructors wear a black sash and practitioners wear the following:

Novices

yellow sash	1st grade
orange sash	2nd grade
green sash	3rd grade
blue sash	4th grade
brown sash	5th grade
black sash	1st degree

Once a practitioner has achieved the black sash, they progress in degrees, which starts at one red band per degree. After achieving 10th degree they can wear a red sash.

white mandarin top

trousers

sashes

3-section staff

siu so gee

black sash

slippers

dip do *knives*

4 red-banded sash

red sash

broad sword

Etiquette

The sign of respect in mok-gar is manifested as a "salute" by practitioners. It is performed at the beginning and end of every session to demonstrate that the practitioner is following the true Shaolin way (having the right attitude and respect towards the art and its beliefs).

1 ◁ Stand in a relaxed position with your hands behind your back. There are no specific rules governing which hand should be over which – it is just a natural standing posture with feet facing forwards, a shoulder-width apart, back straight, shoulders relaxed and eyes looking forwards.

△ Rear view of hand positions.

2 △ Make a fist with your right hand and keep your left hand open with your thumb relaxed. Place your fist into the centre of the palm of your left hand and prepare to move forwards.

3 △ Step forwards with your left foot into the cat stance. At the same time, continue to bring your hands round to the centre of your upper body.

4 △ Side view of the salute position.
Note: this salute is also used before sparring, as a sign of respect to your partner. Following the etiquette, practitioners stand in a relaxed position with their hands behind their back, as depicted in step 1.

Exercise | Warm-up

As with the other disciplines, mok-gar uses a variety of warm-up routines which are designed to prevent injuries during practice. Since this discipline is predominantly centred around leg techniques, leg-stretching exercises are particularly important, focusing on leg muscles, ligaments and tendons.

WARM-UP 1 – *Stretching the leg tendons and hamstring muscles is a vital part of the warm-up.*

WARM-UP 2 – *This exercise stretches the inner thighs and develops good body posture.*

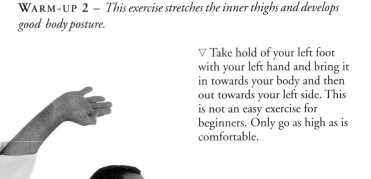

❶ ◁ Raise your leg as high as is comfortable. Gradually build up the tempo and height of the kick. Each exercise is performed by counting from one to ten in Cantonese. Then change to the other leg.

▽ A variation of the front-kick stretching exercise is to kick your leg forwards and outwards in a circular motion. Try to keep the heel of your stationary leg firmly planted on the ground while kicking. If you go up on to your toes you will lose balance. Don't worry about achieving any great height with any kicking or stretching exercise if you are just starting out – it is better to aim for waist level and gradually build up the height.

▽ Take hold of your left foot with your left hand and bring it in towards your body and then out towards your left side. This is not an easy exercise for beginners. Only go as high as is comfortable.

WARM-UP 3 – *Breathing exercises play an important part in mok-gar. The following exercise demonstrates what is known as dynamic tension, which is a body tensing exercise.*

◁ Lower your body into the horse stance, knees bent and with your feet facing forwards. Breathe in slowly through your nose, right down into the pit of your stomach. Hold this for a few seconds and then breathe out slowly through your mouth. While breathing, move both hands in a circular action, first forwards, then back in towards you, finally pushing out to the sides.

WARM-UP 4– *When exercising with a partner, take great care not to stretch him too far. Apply the exercise gently, gradually pushing the leg a little further each time you practise.*

△ Lie down on the floor and allow your partner to secure your right knee and raise your left leg. Keep your leg straight. Your partner then pushes your left leg upwards. Change to the opposite leg and repeat the exercise 3 or 4 times each side.

WARM-UP 5 – *This series of moves is designed to develop your arms.*

❶ △ Gently make contact with your partner's forearms in a rotating action, first left, then right.

❷ △ Bend your arms so that you are now making contact with your partner's upturned fists in line with your chin. As you perform this exercise, try to use hip rotation to enhance the technique.

❸ △ Lower your arms so that you are making contact with the lower part of your partner's forearms. This looks very similar to the first position.

Technique | One-man blocking

The purpose of this technique is to develop basic blocking forms. Each movement is a block towards an on-coming attack. Beginners would learn these basics before starting to work with a partner. The second stage involves the two-man blocking form to develop awareness, timing, distancing and body movement.

1 ◁ Stand in a natural position with your feet together and both fists at your side.

2 △ Keeping your toes together, move your heels outwards.

3 △ Twist on the balls of your feet and then twist your heels as you move into a wider stance. Straighten your toes as you then move outwards.

4 △ Continue to pivot on your heels and toes into a low horse stance. Keep both knees bent. It is important to push your knees outwards.

5 △ Raise your right hand into an upper block position. Keep your left fist and elbow tucked into your side. Look straight ahead and repeat this exercise with the left arm.

6 △ Push your right arm forwards with your right palm moving forwards and upwards. Keep your left fist on your left hip in preparation to move forwards. Ensure you are still in a low horse stance.

7 △ Repeat the exercise with your left arm and follow through with your right. It is important to keep your back straight and maintain the same posture.

8 △ With an open right palm, prepare to block across your body.

9 △ Follow through with a downwards, circular block to your right side. Repeat these moves, reversing hand and arm positions.

10 △ Push both hands forwards, palms upwards and thumbs tucked in.

11 △ Rotate your hands in a circular motion towards your face, keeping your little fingers together to start the rotation movement.

△ The rolling-finger technique seen from the side view.

12 △ Continue to rotate the hands so that they move into the tiger-claw position.

13 △ Defend with your left hand crossing your body. Keep your right hand on your hip and maintain the low horse stance.

14 △ Move your hands into the butterfly position, by crossing your right palm over your left, in preparation to push downwards.

15 △ Push your hand down, keeping your right hand on top.

16 △ Both hands need to be flat as they push down in a circular action. Note the low body position. Ensure your right hand is on top of your left hand, with fingers straight. Draw your left leg up to your right leg and bring your fists back to your waist to finish – this is similar to the starting position.

Technique | Two-man blocking form

The two-man defence form is designed to develop effective blocking and striking techniques. The advantage of using a partner is to promote increased awareness of movement, timing and delivery of the block. Such practice sharpens the ability to focus on a moving target and develop a "feel" for when and how to defend and strike.

1 △ Lower your posture and transfer 70 per cent of your weight on to your back leg. Slightly bend your front knee and keep your toes turned slightly inwards. Place your hands in the guard position with your right hand open. *Note: you can use either hand, depending on the fighting posture adopted.*

2 △ Your opponent delivers a strike to your face. Deflect the attack using an upper-arm block with your left arm. The front arm must always be in a fist position with the rear in an open hand guard.

3 △ Bring your arm back in to your body and bring your left leg up in preparation to strike your opponent in the floating rib.

4 △ Deliver a kick to the floating rib. Ensure that it is the heel of your foot that makes contact, otherwise your kick will be weak and you could hurt your toes. Maintain a good posture and keep looking at your opponent.

Technique | Drilling stance

The drilling stance exercise is designed to improve overall general fitness, flexibility, balance and strength. Regular practice enhances leg mobility and coordination of movement and breathing in preparation to perform many of the skills utilized in mok-gar, including hand and weaponry. Repetition is viewed as important in all basic practice.

1 △ Lower your body into the horse stance and place both fists on your hips. Maintain a low posture and keep looking forwards.

2 △ Turn to the left and move into the bow stance – so called because it echoes the shape of a bow and arrow. Place the fists out forwards (natural, relaxed breathing ensures that the practitioner exhales on the strike). Return to the horse stance and repeat the exercise to the opposite side. Repeat 2 or 3 times each side.

3 △ Move through with your right leg into a forward cat position. Keep your knees well-bent with about 70 per cent of your weight on your rear leg. Your hands should be in the claw style – known as the tiger claw movement. Repeat, moving to your right side.

Technique | Self-defence

Mok-gar utilizes many of the basic techniques and forms into effective self defence applications. The following demonstrates one such application, showing the use of body blocks, hand strikes and leg techniques. Various combination techniques are practised in mok-gar to defend against a variety of attacks to the head and body.

❶ △ Use a lower-forearm block as your opponent moves in with his right hand to strike at your upper body.

❷ △ Take hold of your opponent's right wrist with your right hand.

❸ △ Bring your left hand up in a circular inwards and outwards motion, aiming to strike the aggressor's nose with the back of your knuckles. At this point the aggressor should be disorientated, enabling you to either escape or to further restrain him.

▷ An alternative defensive strike would be to utilize your legs, making contact with the knife edge of your foot. Mok-gar is well-known for its front kicking strikes (sickle kicks).

Mok-gar utilizes a variety of weapons, many of which are unique to the art, and were adapted from agricultural tools. They were used by farmers to protect their family and land. Today, these weapons are used to maintain the tradition of mok-gar, which practitioners learn as they progress through the art, and they are seen as an extension of the hand.

TEE CHEC – metal bat

△This is a classical pose using the *tee chec*. Here, a block and striking action, taken from a *mok-gar* form (a set of pre-designed moves), is being illustrated.

PEGS – two small rounded pieces of wood

△This weapon gets its name of "the peg" because of its similarity to a wooden dowel. The pegs are principally used to strike at an aggressor's vulnerable spots, such as the mandible, limbs and pressure points.

DIP DO – butterfly knives

△ Illustrating the *dip do* (butterfly knives).

SIU SO GEE – two pieces of wood joined together by a metal chain

△ This shows the *siu so gee* in action. The history of the *siu so gee* begins with a legend that an unknown instructor broke one of his favourite fighting sticks. He was so attached to this particular weapon that he continued to use it, even though it was broken. In this way he developed the shorter stick into a weapon in its own right. The *siu so gee* is sometimes referred to as the "little sweeper".

△ Demonstrating the *siu so gee* as an effective blocking weapon.

THREE-SECTION STAFF – *This was developed as a battlefield weapon and proved particularly useful against cavalry.*

▷ The three-section staff is a complex weapon to use, but very effective in both close and long-range combat. When fully extended it has a 9 ft (2.75 m) range. At close quarters, it can be used for choking and striking, as well as for hooking other weapons to disarm an opponent.

KICK BOXING

功夫

history *and* philosophy

Kick boxing is a relatively modern martial arts system, whose syllabus was derived by combining several fighting techniques from a variety of the more traditional disciplines, including kung fu, kyokushinkai karate, Thai boxing, kyokky shinkai and tae kwondo.

Martial arts boomed during the early 1970s and interest was greatly increased by their emphasis on competition fighting. Chinese styles of fighting began to take on a more Westernized form in the UK, and even more so in the United States, where the first real freestyle systems were beginning to be developed. Indeed, many people claim that kick boxing originated in the US during the 1970s. This, they say, was due to various American karate practitioners becoming frustrated with the limitations of tournament competitive scoring. While karate and the other disciplines were viewed as being entrenched with theories and set *kata*,

Training with hand-held equipment and protective gear is essential if practitioners plan to take their skill into the ring.

Demonstrating superb leg control and posture when striking to the head.

and were performed in a controlled environment, practitioners wanted to see how effective their moves would be in a more realistic environment. Great emphasis began to be placed on specialized techniques, such as kicks and punches, being delivered with full force. Although full-contact karate was already established, concerns were

expressed for the safety of competitors. The first tournament stars of kick boxing were Bill "Superfoot" Wallis, Demetrius Havanas, Joe Lewis, Jeff Smith and Benny Urquidez.

Initially, some people felt that kick boxing looked amateurish, and questioned its validity as a traditional martial art. It is viewed by many as a sport that is a relatively

As with conventional boxing, full contact kick boxing tournaments are conducted in a boxing ring environment.

new discipline and has yet to establish long-term traditions and history.

The World Kick Boxing Association (known as the WKA) apparently came into being in the early 1970s following a tournament with Benny Urquidez, who was sent to Japan to represent America in a kick boxing championship. He won his first world title in 1974. Although many other kick boxing representatives were defeated, Urquidez was able to hold his own, and he was successful to some extent because of his research into Eastern training methods and his well-developed boxing and judo skills. One memorable bout was against the renowned Fujiwara, who was skilled in both karate and Thai boxing.

There is a close affinity between kick boxing and Thai boxing. While it is believed that the Americans had created this concept in their attempt to find a sport that could refine full-contact competition, it is believed that the development of kick boxing was borne out of the WKA finding common ground between Eastern and Western fighting culture.

It is also believed that Joe Cawley and Don and Judy Quinn, along with Howard Hansen, a shorin ryu karate black belt, were the initial promoters of kick boxing and worked together for improved recognition. Hansen took kick boxing a stage further, by introducing fights in a boxing ring, rather than the usual karate tournament bouts. He became known as a ring matchmaker, staging a variety of successful events with such stars as Bill "Superfoot" Wallis.

New rules evolved and were introduced into kick boxing, most notably weight divisions – from fly weight to heavy weight – similar to those in orthodox boxing.

A down-side to the discipline in those early days was criticism of a high risk of injury. This led to improvement in the safety rules, such as contestants wearing protective clothing to cushion the impact of blows. When wearing protective clothing, there are two main fighting distinctions: semi-contact and full contact.

Semi-contact is where two fighters are allowed "reasonable", light contact in an attempt to score points off each other, in the same way as fencing. Full contact is usually fought under the same conditions as a standard boxing match, in which a knock-out is the ultimate aim. Individual clubs compete at inter-club competitions or in open, national

Protective clothing or not, care and caution are always of paramount importance.

In Thailand many fights end this way!

and international, martial arts tournaments. Women do not generally compete against men, but women's kick boxing competitions are becoming more common.

Rules vary, but more recently tournament organizers have insisted on competitors wearing full protective clothing, for even in "semi-contact with control" bouts, injuries can still occur. Men are expected to wear a head guard, gum shield, groin guard, shin, hand and foot pads. Women are expected to wear the same, except that the groin guard is swapped for a chest guard. These rules apply to children.

The order of belts (representing degrees of proficiency) are: white, yellow, orange, blue, green, purple, brown and black. Once the black-belt level has been achieved, progression to a higher grade is through degrees of *dan*, signified by a stripe in the belt – for example, a 1st-*dan* practitioner is entitled to wear a black belt containing one stripe.

Although traditional moves are not really taught, there are set moves that practitioners need to acquire in order to attain each belt. These include hand and kick blocks, shadow boxing, sparring, kicks, punches and wood breaking.

Caution: any breaking techniques must be supervised by an instructor. Never try to perform breaking techniques without professional guidance, as serious injury may

result. Injuries may be immediate or take years to become apparent, but the risk is very real. It is an aggressive sport, but as with most other martial arts disciplines, the true kick boxer is less likely to initiate or be involved in violence, preferring to walk away from a difficult situation.

BENEFITS OF KICK BOXING

There are numerous benefits derived from learning kick boxing, which extend into many aspects of everyday life. These include:

- Appeals to both men and women, irrespective of occupation or level of fitness
- Develops strength and flexibility
- Improves mental agility and stamina
- Powerful and skilful sport
- Increases confidence
- Promotes fitness and well-being
- Reduces stress
- Promotes comradeship
- Assists with self-defence skills

clothing *and*
equipment

The clothing of kick boxing practitioners can vary from club to club. Designs are similar and usually consist of a comfortable top and elasticated trousers. Any colour is acceptable. In view of the emphasis on controlled fighting (sparring), it is very important to wear protective clothing and equipment. Protective equipment must be checked regularly to prevent any unnecessary injury to either the practitioner or their partner.

Loose cotton top, which will depict the colours of the style and club.

Elasticated trousers, which are usually white or black with a stripe identifying the style and club.

ORDER OF KICK BOXING GRADES

Beginner	White
Beginner	Yellow
Junior	Orange
Junior	Green
Intermediate	Blue
Intermediate	Purple
Senior	Brown
1st degree	Black
2nd degree	Black
3rd degree	Black

Protective head-guard and gloves for full contact sparring. The head-guard must fit securely.

Padded footwear to protect both the practitioner and his/her partner during kicking strikes.

Etiquette

Etiquette in kick boxing is used at the beginning of a practice session, when training with a partner and when competing in a tournament. As with other disciplines, the style and form of the etiquette is used as a sign of respect towards your partner or opponent. There is only one bow, as shown.

READY POSITION

1 ◁ Stand with an upright posture – back straight and eyes looking forward. Ensure your shoulders are relaxed and stomach muscles firm. Turn your hands into fists by curling the fingers (starting with the little finger). Place your thumb securely on top of your fingers and position both hands in front of your body. Make sure your elbows are tucked in and feet comfortably astride. Bend both knees slightly and keep your elbows close in to your waist, to ensure there are no vulnerable areas where an opponent could strike. Maintain an inner calm while adopting an assertive, well-focused attitude towards your training partner.

2 ◁ Lower your body, keeping your elbows well tucked in. Perform a bow at about 30 degrees without taking your eyes off your partner.

FIGHTING STANCE

▽ Move forwards from the ready position, using your preferred leg and with your fists raised. Keep your elbows close to your body and your fists clenched. Keep your guard up in front of your body as a protective measure, to deflect or strike, as required. In this side view you can see the correct upright posture and the angle of the fists. Fists that are too high increase the vulnerability of your lower body; if they are too low, your face is at risk. The centre-body position offers the best overall protection.

Exercise | Warm-up

Exercises in kick boxing are designed to improve stamina and enhance flexibility, working towards the goal of toning and strengthening the body and increasing mental agility. Below is a selection of the more important exercises used in warm-up sessions, prior to basic practice. There is particular emphasis on leg stretching and stamina building.

WARM-UP 1 – *This exercise is excellent for stretching the spine and increasing general flexibility.*

1 △ Lie down on a flat, comfortable surface and slightly raise your knees off the floor. Place your hands at the side of your head.

2 △ Keeping your hands lightly at the side of your head, raise your torso while pulling your knees up and into your chest. Lie back down without letting your feet or head touch the ground and repeat 4 or 5 times.

WARM-UP 2 – *This exercise is called the horse-riding stance, because of its obvious resemblance to a figure seated on a horse. It is intended to strengthen buttocks, inner thighs, triceps and biceps.*

WARM-UP 3 – *This exercise needs to be performed slowly and gently, to allow yourself to become supple naturally . It stretches and strengthens the hamstrings and needs to be practised regularly.*

△ With your legs stretched fairly wide, bend your knees while keeping your back straight. Thrust your left fist out in front of your body in a striking position and place your right fist on your hip, touching your waistline. Hold this position for about 60–90 seconds. Alternate with your opposite fist and repeat 4 or 5 times.

△ Let your partner take hold of your leg at the ankle and gently raise it, stopping periodically to ensure you are comfortable. Your partner, in an upright position, needs to gently raise your leg. Keep a straight back leg and upright posture. Hold for 20–30 seconds and repeat 3 to 4 times each side.

WARM-UP 4 – *It is important to perform this exercise sensibly, with both partners working together. You will cause unnecessary pain if you push down too heavily, without regard for your partner's level of flexibility.*

△ Lie on your back and place your hands either at the sides of your body or lightly on your stomach. Let your legs fall apart and keep your breathing slow and calm. Your partner then gently pushes down on your inner thighs, stretching your legs apart, for approximately 60 seconds.

WARM-UP 5 – *This exercise assists in strengthening both the stomach muscles and lower back of both practitioners. Mutual cooperation is important to ensure maximum benefit and safety.*

△ Lie on your back and bring your knees into your chest. Place your hands, palms down, on the floor at your sides (experienced people may prefer to rest their hands on their thighs). Allow your standing partner to lean forwards at 45 degrees, resting her stomach on the soles of your feet with hands clasped behind her back. Both partners need to keep the stomach muscles tense. Hold for 20–30 seconds and swop positions. As your strength increases, extend the exercise period, staying within the limits of what feels comfortable to you.

WARM-UP 6 – *This exercise seeks to strengthen the upper body muscles through the application of mild resistance against your partner's applied reasonable pressure.*

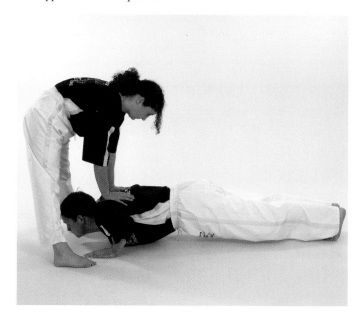

△ Lie face down on the floor in a press-up position with feet together, hands flat and back straight. With your partner's hands on your shoulder applying gentle downward pressure, push your body up by straightening your elbows. Relax for a few seconds after each press-up. Repeat the exercise no more than 5 times in a session. Change roles and repeat.

WARM-UP 7 – *This wheelbarrow press-up is an advanced exercise for more experienced practitioners. It is good for developing the top part of the body, including the triceps, biceps and abdomen.*

△ Go into the usual press-up position and then let your partner take hold of and raise your ankles to waist level. Push down to perform the press-ups, ensuring maximum pressure on the upper part of your body, while your partner continues to hold your legs by the ankles. Then lower your body towards the floor and do not let your face make contact with the ground. Push down as near to the floor as you can. Finally, push your body up from the floor as high as you can and then clap your hands before going back down. Perform this exercise fairly slowly and no more than 10 times.

Technique | Fighting stance

The fighting stance is used when practising techniques with a partner and in preparation for sparring. If your partner is not wearing correct body and head protection, as in the case of practising basic techniques, it is important to make sure you do not make actual contact. Aim to focus your strikes at 1 in (2. 5 cm) away from the target area.

❶ ◁ With your feet shoulder-width apart, step back into the ready position and assume the guard position. With your preferred leg forwards place your feet firmly on the floor with your front foot facing forwards and the rear foot at an angle of about 45 degrees. Keep your eyes forward and fixed on your partner.

❷ ▷ As your partner moves in to strike your face with a left punch, maintain your body position and perform an upward rising block (known as an upper block) with your left arm. Keep your right fist at your hip, ready to perform a counter-strike. Maintain a good posture and keep your eyes on your partner.

❸ ▷ You can now perform a variety of counter-strikes. As the left arm block exposes your partner's body, perform a right-hand punch to the solar plexus. Make sure your blocking arm is pulled back, since this punching technique takes advantage of the extra power delivered as you swing your hips around behind the blow.

△ Alternative counter-strikes can be seen in close-up. First, a back fist strike to the temple. Make sure your fist is tightly closed with the thumb locked on top.

△ Second, a ridge hand blow to the temple. Tuck the thumb into the centre of your palm and keep your fingers straight. Deliver this blow by making a large circular action from the centre of your body to enhance the power of the strike.

BASIC
Technique | Side kick

Side kicks are difficult to block and are very effective in sparring, especially in competition, where the aim is to score points. The body is turned to the side, having the advantage of making the practitioner a smaller target. The knife edge of the foot is the striking area which makes contact.

1 ▷ Lift your knee high, as close to your chest as you can. Point your toes downwards and keep your hand guard in the front position. Your back foot must be firmly placed flat on the floor – avoid lifting the heel since this will take you off balance.

2 △ Perform a side kick by extending your raised leg, turning the toes inwards so that the side of the foot (the knife edge) makes contact. Try to maintain a good, upright posture to assist your balance. Keep your guard hands up and maintain focus on your partner.

3 △ Complete the practice by bringing your kicking foot back again. Maintain the same hand guard position. This requires strength and control and it minimizes the risk of your leg being grabbed when extended and in a self-defence situation. (In competition, if the leg is not pulled back no points are scored). Bring the kicking foot back down to the floor in preparation to begin again.

Technique | Self-defence

Many people take up a martial art as a self-defence measure. Kick boxing utilizes various self-defence moves, and the following technique is just one example of the many strategies that are suitable for both men and women, when seeking to learn self-protection. Physical defence is only used as a last resort, when all else has failed.

1 ◁ Stand in the ready position with your fists at waist level. Your opponent adopts a fighting posture.

2 ▷ Your opponent moves in with a side-kicking attack.

3 ◁ You move 45 degrees to the right (away from the kicking leg) and then move back in with a hooking block. This is immediately followed by a punch to either the upper body or head region.

△ The close-up view shows how the hooking block works. This is achieved by using a scooping motion to sweep the attacking leg, and then control the opponent's body, by immediately securing the leg in towards your body. This puts the opponent in a very vulnerable position, where it is difficult for him to maintain balance with only one foot in the air.

4 ▽ You can now perform a leg sweep to unbalance your opponent by bringing your right leg around his leg. *Note: it is important to continue securing the opponent's right leg to maintain control of the technique. This technique is only used in self-defence practice.*

◁ This close-up shows your hand position on your opponent's shoulder, ready to push him forwards and downwards on to the floor. It is important to hold on to your opponent when practising this technique, by taking hold of his clothing on the right or left shoulder.

5 ◁ Once your opponent is on the floor, start to move your head and body to the side and out of reach, so that you cannot be grabbed and pulled to the floor. Maintain a good stance and posture to help you avoid losing your balance and falling down with your opponent.

6 ▷ A variety of finishing techniques can be applied, ranging from punching to kicking. Ideally a kicking technique is useful, as it enables you to maintain a safer distance.

Technique | Contact sparring

Contact sparring is a fundamental element of kick boxing. Respect and control of the techniques is of paramount importance, to maintain safety. It is commonplace for men and women to practise with each other, although in the competition environment sexes are usually demarcated. The following demonstrates one basic routine.

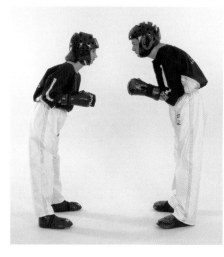

❶ △ Stand opposite your partner, making sure you maintain focus. Keep your guard up and your feet a shoulder-width apart. An inner sense of assertion and control is vital. Stand about one and a half arm's length away from your partner, in readiness to commence sparring. If you are too close you increase your vulnerability to being punched or kicked.

❷ △ Perform a bow by lowering the top part of your body by about 30 degrees. Maintain your guard by keeping your eyes fixed on your partner.

❸ △ Move into fighting posture by touching gloves. This is a sign of respect, indicating that although you intend to go into a fighting situation, you are still showing sportsmanship and friendship.

❺ △ If you manage to block a kick or punch, try to score a point by punching the body or head region.

❹ △ The object of the sparring is to increase speed and agility. As one partner may try to score a point with a kick, the other must try to block. Note the good upright posture when kicking and the guard being kept in place in preparation for a counter-attack.

COMPETITION TECHNIQUES
It is important that you use the correct protective equipment – head padding, body armour, shin, hand and foot protection – in competition. Both partners will wear gum shields, and men must wear groin guards and women chest guards. It is very important that you show respect towards your partner. Sparring should not be seen as an opportunity to hurt somebody.

COMPETITION
Technique | Close punching

The following examples demonstrate a variety of close punching techniques. A particular style of punching in kick boxing is the uppercut punch. It is important to practise these techniques under proper supervision from a qualified instructor, and while wearing the correct protective clothing.

❶ ◁ A round-house hook to the side of the head. This is a hook, demonstrates an effective strike to a vulnerable area of the head e.g. hinge of jaw (mandible) and therefore warrants points.

❷ ▷ An uppercut to the chin. This strike has to be delivered at close range and could follow a number of other striking techniques. As with all striking techniques which make contact, an opening has been created, either by the partner letting his guard down, or their position inviting an opportunity to strike at a vulnerable area.

❸ ▽ A straight punch to the body. As your partner's guard has moved, a vulnerable area has been exposed, which creates an opportunity to strike the solar plexus or stomach region, for example.

CAUTION

Whilst partners wear protective equipment, a degree of caution is still exercised through the sensible application of punching techniques. Remember: when sparring, partners are moving around, which requires skills in distancing and focusing. It is easy to hit an accessible partner, and therefore the skill lies in effective control and discipline of movement.

COMPETITION
Technique | Blocking

As part of defensive manoeuvres, blocking plays an important role. The following demonstrates a variety of blocking techniques which can be employed against different attacks. Leg movements feature predominantly in kick boxing and are difficult to block, as the legs are the most powerful striking tool.

△ A double-handed block to defend against a kick to the body.

△ An open-handed block to defend against a circular leg strike.

△ A defence against a head attack, using an upper block.

△ An outward-hooking block to a leg attack.

Technique | Kicking techniques

The following demonstrates some of the kicking techniques that can be included in competition and in advanced practice. The top two pictures display kicks that can score points in competition fighting, while the two pictures along the bottom demonstrate more advanced techniques that are not usually allowed in competition sparring.

△ A head kick being counter-attacked by an upper-head block.

△ A spinning back kick into the solar plexus region.

△ A flying side kick, known as a "jump or flying technique", achieved by jumping, turning and kicking your partner while in mid air. A jump kick is to the body while a flying kick is to the head.

△ A flying front kick.

SCORES

In competition, points are awarded for particular techniques, with extra points being scored for more complicated and difficult manoeuvres such as combination techniques.

Points can vary, but the standard scoring system is usually:

one point for a hand technique to the body or head

two points for a leg technique to the body

three points for a leg technique to the head.

TAI CHI CHUAN

Tai chi chuan combines the *yin* and *yang* approach of serene movements for health and well-being with a strong fighting system of self-defence. It is an excellent discipline for people of all ages and abilities, including children as young as five years of age. Older people also benefit fron tai chi chuan, such as the 81-year-old Chinese Grand Master Jiang Hao Quan, who is convinced that his youthful appearance, healthy mind and body are all due to his tai chi chuan training.

TAI CHI CHUAN

太極拳

history *and* philosophy

The initial aim of tai chi chuan is to teach the practitioner to relax. "Relax" in this sense does not mean to flop loosely around, but rather to use the body as efficiently as possible, with no muscular tension. The foremost requirement is good posture with relaxed shoulders, an upright back and firmly rooted stance. Tai chi chuan incorporates chi kung exercises, which encourage deep breathing, improved blood circulation and greater efficiency of the body's systems. On a mental level, the quiet concentration required for tai chi chuan brings a serene state of mind, in which the everyday stresses of life can be placed in their proper perspective. This

Chang San Feng, the legendary founder of tai chi chuan.

leads to a more tolerant, even state of mind, and a calm mind is able to respond more quickly and effectively to challenges in any situation.

At this level, the art is accessible to anyone – age, health or infirmity are not barriers to reaping some of the rewards that tai chi chuan has to offer. However, to reach the higher levels it is necessary to study the art in its wider context. Practising the martial aspects of tai chi chuan involves more complex forms of chi kung, body strengthening, two-person practice and various supplementary exercises. Such training is more demanding than basic-form practice, but it does bring greater benefits in terms of mental and physical health, as well as providing an excellent self-defence method. At the higher stages the theoretical aspects of the art also become more apparent.

As a martial art, tai chi chuan works on a number of levels, but the principal aim is to teach practitioners to relax and become fluid in their movements. This allows for smoother actions and quicker response times. The objective is for self-defence to become a reflexive action rather than a repetition of technique. There is a variety of sensitivity exercises which allow the practitioner to adapt instantly to an opponent and to react in the most appropriate manner. Incoming force will, typically, be diverted, however slightly, and the corresponding opening in the opponent's defence exploited. The level of response can range from applying

The tranquillity of early morning practice.

Practice in public places is not uncommon.

locks and holds, to immobilizing an opponent, through to highly damaging strikes against nerve centres and acupuncture points (*dim mak*).

The origins

Tai chi chuan is usually translated into English as "the supreme ultimate fist". The term *tai chi* refers to the *yin-yang* symbol prevalent in Chinese culture, more commonly known as the "hard" and "soft" sign – the two opposites coming together. The term *chuan* refers to a boxing method – boxing in this context means a method of empty-hand combat, rather than a sporting contest. Thus, as the name suggests, tai chi chuan is a self-defence method, one that is based on the Chinese Taoist philosophy of life.

Tai chi chuan is also referred to as internal kung fu. The reference to "internal" here refers to the general rule that tai chi emphasizes the development of the internal aspects of the body – breathing, flexibility and the mind – as opposed to external tension or muscular strength.

The roots of tai chi chuan are enshrouded in myth, and all but lost in legend, but the most popular theory refers to the art being originated by Chang San Feng, who was born in 1247. Chang studied at the famous Shaolin temple and mastered its system of martial arts. He then travelled to Wutang Mountain, a region populated by Taoist hermits where, as the legend goes, Chang watched as a stork and a snake fought. Fascinated by the fluidity of their movements and their ability both to evade and attack simultaneously, Chang adapted his system to incorporate the movements he had witnessed. It is also said that Chang had developed a high degree of skill in striking the body's acupuncture points, which he also incorporated into his art, though heavily disguised.

Yang Lu Chan (1799–1872), the undefeated founder of the Yang Family tai chi chuan.

Flowing and serene movement in group practice.

This art was passed down in great secrecy for many generations, eventually reaching the Wang family. The Wang family passed it on to the Chen family, who absorbed it into their own system, known as *pao chuan* (meaning "cannon fist"). The art at this stage was not called tai chi chuan: that name came to be applied only many years later. The Chens were held in high regard for their martial prowess and this attracted Yang Lu Chan (1799-1872) to the Chen village. The art was still being taught in great secrecy but, through his dedication, Yang was able to learn from the head of the style, Chen Chan Hsing. Then, after a short period of studying with the Wang family, Yang travelled to the imperial capital of Peking.

Once in Peking, Yang met many challengers from other styles of martial art, but remained undefeated, earning the nickname "Invincible Yang". Due to his reputation, Yang was ordered to teach the imperial family and the Manchu imperial bodyguard. It was impossible to ignore such a decree, yet Yang taught just a part of the art to the unpopular Manchu, retaining the knowledge of the complete system only for close family and trusted students.

Tai chi chuan's popularity began to spread among the nobility of the day and Yang's sons, both of whom were formidable fighters, continued this process, although the art was to some extent modified to suit the less rigorous lifestyles of the rich.

Transitionary process

It was during the 1920s that tai chi chuan really began to spread to different parts of the country. China at that time was in turmoil, with the population sick and ailing. The health benefits of the art became recognized and the once-secret art of the Chen family became a national exercise. You should note, however, that the art in its more popular form contains only part of the training of the traditional family styles, which, even today, are taught only to close students in order to maintain their secrecy and discretion. The main family styles – Chen, Yang, Hao and Wu – form the basis for many variations of style and form. Since the 1960s the art, in many guises, has spread to the West, making it a truly global phenomenon and the most widely practised martial art in the world.

Conclusion

Power training consists of chi kung to develop internal strength, as well as methods to strengthen the tendons and ligaments. The ability to issue power (*fa jing*) from close range is a primary feature of tai chi chuan. This involves incorporating the whole body into one unit behind an attack. Tai chi chuan includes punches, kicks, locks, open-hand techniques and throws in its repertoire, as well as traditional Chinese weapons: sword, broadsword, staff and spear.

Today, while traditional practitioners of tai chi chuan are still in evidence, the majority practise the art in order to both maintain and improve their health and to provide an increasingly necessary antidote to the stresses and strains of modern-day life.

BENEFITS OF TAI CHI CHUAN

- Enhances the ability of the practitioner to maintain an inner calm
- Enhances motivation and performance in all areas of life, such as work, social and home life
- Increases flexibility of muscles and movement of the body
- Increases quality of life through the "inner-calmness" approach to difficult situations
- Works towards a healthy mind and body, which can slow down the ageing process
- Reduces stress by increased awareness of relaxation skills

- Reduces tension through the development of inner energy and calmness of mind
- Reduces the need for other stimulants, such as alcohol and drugs
- Develops deep concentration and mental focus
- Assists in calming breathing and heart and brain processes, which can help our emotional responses to situations
- Assists the flow of energy in the body, thereby reducing both mental and physical blockages
- Improves the sense of humour

clothing *and* equipment

The traditional clothing and equipment for tai chi chuan is much the same as that for other Chinese martial arts: a black mandarin suit, flat-bottomed shoes and the traditional weapons – staff, sword, broad sword and spear. Generally speaking, class students wear any suitable loose clothing. Traditional uniforms are usually reserved for special occasions and public demonstrations.

Other than this, there are also various types of equipment available, such as focus pads and kick bags used in self-defence training, or for various supplementary exercises, such as grip training and body conditioning. Protective clothing may be worn in some instances, such as for students who are just beginning to spar.

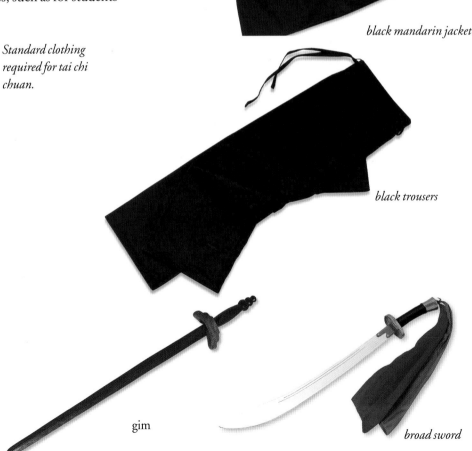

black mandarin jacket

black trousers

gim

broad sword

Standard clothing required for tai chi chuan.

Etiquette

Etiquette is important within most martial arts disciplines and is carried out as a sign of respect. For example, the following moves are performed at the beginning and the end of the training session, and before practising with a partner. This is a traditional tai chi chuan salute.

1 ◁ Stand in a relaxed position with your feet together and hands at your side. Keep your back straight and shoulders relaxed. Clear your mind and try to induce a feeling of inner calm.

❷ △ Bring both hands up in front of your chest, making your right hand into a fist and keeping the left hand open, fingers together. Place your right hand in the palm of the left and keep your eyes looking forwards.

❸ △ Make a 30-degree bow forwards, keeping your hands together and eyes looking forwards. This is done to show respect to the art and the ancestors of tai chi chuan and to your training partner during practice.

△ This profile view of the bow shows that the position of your arms is slightly extended forward. Move back into the upright position, ready to commence practice.

Exercise | Warm-up

Most exercises are performed gently and slowly to maintain a feeling of inner calm, while stretching and strengthening the body. The following demonstrates two warm-up exercises that are usually performed before practising the basic techniques. The purpose of the exercises is to promote suppleness and flexibility within the body.

WARM-UP 1 – *This exercise has been developed to help make the waist, hips and the lower back region more supple.*

①△ Stand upright with both hands cupped together and your thumbs touching. Bend your knees slightly to lower your posture. Both feet should be facing forwards. Place your left thumb on top of your right.

②△ Pull your left hand around the side of your body, with the right hand following in a flowing action. Make sure you keep your feet facing forwards as your hands move around your body in a circular motion.

③△ Draw your hands backwards in a circular motion, ensuring that your palms are always facing upwards, almost as if you are holding a small bowl, and then start to move your hands in front of your body.

④△ Continuing the flowing movement, bring your hands slowly and gently in front of the body. Breathe naturally throughout the exercise.

⑤◁ Continue the flowing action, with your left hand moving across the body towards your head.

⑥▷ Lean backwards from the waist, flexing your stomach muscles to strengthen and increase flexibility. From this position rotate the upper part of the body and then resume the original starting position.

△ This side view demonstrates the correct arch of the body.

WARM-UP 2 – *This exercise is designed to strengthen the arms and requires the controlled breathing described below.*

❶ △ Stand in the ready position with your feet a shoulder-width apart. Make both hands into fists by your hips, palms upwards. Make sure your posture is upright, knees are slightly bent and your feet are facing forwards.

❷ △ Slowly push your right fist forwards while exhaling. As you bring your fist back to the hip, inhale slowly. Perform this action slowly and with focus.

❸ △ Repeat the previous action, this time using your left fist, remembering to maintain the correct breathing pattern.

◁ This view shows the slightly bent knees and correct, upright posture.

❹ ▷ After performing this exercise several times, return both fists to your hips and bring your feet together.

Technique | Hook

A popular technique in tai chi chuan is known as *tan pien*, or the "hook" position. This technique has various applications, namely a strike using the back of the hand, wrist strike, striking with the fingers, blocking or breaking a gripping technique. This technique assists in opening the joints and stretching the tendons, to increase strength and flexibility.

❶ ◁ Adopt a forwards stance with your left palm pushing forwards at chest height and your right arm extended to the rear with the hand in the hook position. Ensure that 70 per cent of your weight is on your front leg in preparation to move backwards.

▷ Note the angle of the hand and the fingertips touching in this detail of the hook position.

❷ ▷ The rear foot turns outwards and the weight begins to move on to the back leg. This is a smooth and continuous motion. The left hand begins to drop as if blocking a striking technique.

❸ ▷ This is the "snake creeps down" (*hsia shih*) position and it requires you to manoeuvre your body. Lower your posture by bending your back (right) leg so that your upper and lower leg form a 90-degree angle. Transfer about 70 per cent of your body weight on to your right leg. Keeping your back straight and eyes fixed on your imaginary opponent, slide your left arm down your left leg, palm uppermost and fingers outstretched.

Technique | Striking

In this exercise you need the assistance of a partner, who assumes the role of an aggressor and prepares to strike you. Here, tai chi chuan employs techniques in a continuous flow to successfully defend against an aggressive strike. The following demonstrates the method of moving in from medium distance to close range.

1 △ While it could be argued that in a street situation an aggressor might not approach you in quite this fashion, it is important when learning and practising techniques that safety and basic movements are applied to learn distancing and timing.

2 △ In this situation the aggressor has thrown a punch. Note how the defender adopts the hooking technique, described earlier in this chapter, and applies it as self-defence in a circular blocking and striking action. Fluidity and timing are very important for this technique to be applied successfully.

3 △ The defender aims to strike the temple. Note how the fingers are pushed together, with the thumb locked, while the back of the hand makes contact on the temple region.

4 △ The defender moves through, with his left leg across the aggressor's right leg, and applies his right hand around the throat, while the left hand is placed on the side of the aggressor's body.

5 ▷ An alternative finishing position is to move in as in step 3, but to place the right hand around the back of the aggressor's neck, aiming for the pressure point that will render the aggressor unconscious. Energy is then directed forwards and downwards to take the aggressor down to the floor.

△ Demonstrating the correct hand position for accuracy on the pressure point.

Technique | Locking and striking

When practising with a partner, set techniques have been developed to enhance body distance and mental awareness. This technique enhances the skill of developing fluidity of movement from striking to grappling with an aggressor. While the movements look relaxing, the energy and skill applied make for an effective method of self-defence.

1 ◁ As the defender in this exercise, you should adopt a more relaxed stance and alert demeanour than that shown by the aggressor, who has both fists forwards. Transfer about 70 per cent of your weight on to the back leg. Keep your left hand in the open position, palm forwards, in front of your chest. Your right hand covers the lower part of your body, ready to deflect a blow.

2 △ Using a circular action with your arms, turn your hips forwards, towards the aggressor, to support a blocking action. Block the punch with the outside of your right forearm. This is known as the "ward-off", or "*p'eng*". Your left hand is positioned either to apply another defensive move or a strike.

3 ▽ Strike with the heel of your left palm into the pressure point on the side of the aggressor's right ribs.

△ Showing the correct hand position to maintain close contact.

4 △ Pull your right hand up and over the aggressor's striking fist. At the same time, bring your left hand along to the aggressor's elbow position. Then push down on the aggressor's pressure point at the elbow, while simultaneously pushing the aggressor's arm forwards and away from his face. This locks the wrist in position and restrains the aggressor. At this point, bring your right leg completely around the aggressor's right leg, in preparation to apply a throwing technique.

Technique | Escape – rear defence

Many people fear being grabbed from the rear, especially around the throat. The following movement describes one of the many defences that can be applied to release such an attack, followed by an effective restraint. This demonstrates the effective self-defence element in tai chi chuan.

❶ △ In this scenario, an attacker has grabbed you around the throat with his left arm, taking hold of your right wrist with his right hand.

❷ △Bring your free left hand up and take hold of the aggressor's left hand at your throat, aiming for the pressure point that is situated between the thumb and the forefinger. At the same time, step back with your right foot and bend forwards to start to unbalance the aggressor.

△ Make sure that you take a firm grip of the aggressor's hand as you start to pull the hand and arm away from your throat. Step backwards also, to prepare for the full disengagement.

❸ △ Pull your body forwards in a downwards motion, at the same time pulling your left hand down and your right arm across your body. This pulls the opponent further off balance. Note that your rear leg is straight and your front leg is bent at 90 degrees.

❹ △With the aggressor now unbalanced, use your elbow to aim a blow at his solar plexus. Now bring your right leg behind the aggressor's left leg in preparation to perform an arm restrain. Push his left arm over your head into a locking position, maintaining a low posture by ensuring a good bend on your left leg and keeping your back leg straight.

❺ △ Push the aggressor's left arm down, making sure that the arm is straight by securely holding the wrist with your left hand and placing your right hand in an upwards fist position, against the aggressor's arm.

❻ ▽ Continue to apply pressure as you push the aggressor to the floor.

Technique | Pushing hands

There are various types of sensitivity training, and the most well-known is pushing hands (*toi sau*). The following is just one example of a basic technique of the pushing hands method for which tai chi chuan is famous. *Toi sau* develops the practitioner's awareness, sensitivity, skills and anticipation of an opponent's movement.

1 ◁ As you can see, the age, height and gender of the partners in this exercise are irrelevant. Here, the woman (partner 1) places her right hand, palm inwards, in the defensive "ward-off" position against the man's (partner 2) open-hand, forwards position.

2 ▷ Partner 2 pushes partner 1's hand towards her chest area. She deflects the push by turning and performing a circular action.

3 △ Partner 1 continues the circular action in a flowing motion, pushing forwards. It is very much like a circular, flowing action, twisting the side of the hand and the palm around. Partner 1 is now pushing towards partner 2's chest in a reversal of the original stance.

4 ▷ Partner 2 now allows the circular action to go across his partner's body and towards the right side, preparing to push back into the centre as a prelude to repeating the whole exercise.

Tai chi chuan utilizes a variety of weapons, including straight sword, staff and broad sword/sabre. Below are a sample of some of the moves taken from various *kata*, or sequences of set moves, demonstrating the use of the swords in both defensive and striking actions.

▷ This balanced stance is known as "lifting the leg to pierce" and it is used in a stabbing action.

△ "Drift with the current." This is a slicing action to the lower leg.

▽ The broad sword is kept out of view in preparation to strike. This technique is known as "conceal the sabre to kick".

△ This technique is known as the "big dipper" and is used when the practitioner is blocking with the straight sword and preparing to strike with the left leg.

△ "Turning the sword/sabre to pierce."

KENDO

On first impressions, kendo appears to be very physical and aggressive, with the dynamics of a fast-striking action and high-pitched screams. Yet it is an art that places great emphasis on the development of a high level of skill in concentration, timing, awareness, physical agility, footwork, body movement and inherent respect. Kendo was derived from the ancient art of Japanese *samurai* swordsmanship. Armour is worn for protection, and a sword made of four sections of bamboo is bound together to make what is known as a *shinai*.

剣
道

KENDO

history *and* philosophy

Kenjutsu is the earliest martial art, dating back to before 1590, followed by kendo, which had more intellectual and philosophical characteristics. Kenjutsu became modern kendo, which has developed a sport-orientated nature that still embodies many of the traditional values.

It is believed that the origins of kenjutsu are located in the classical Chinese era, which dates back more than 2,000 years. However, while kendo is very much a modern art that has been influenced by kenjutsu, its roots can be traced back as far back as AD 789 through the history of the art of the sword which is linked inextricably to the history of ancient Japan. It was at this time that *Komutachi*, the sword exercise, was introduced as an instruction for the sons of the *kuge* (noblemen) in the city of Nara, then the capital of Japan.

Today's kendo very much relates to the changes in swordsmanship that came about in the early Tokugawa period of around 1600–1750. At this time, Japan embarked on an increasing period of stability, and the change from kenjutsu to kendo took place. It was not until the end of the 18th century, however, that the *shinai* (bamboo stick) became commonly used in basic practice. *Kendoka* (kendo students) would also work with the *bokken* (a wooden replica of a sword) and the *katana* (a practice sword).

It is interesting to note that, for the greatest part of Japanese history, kendo and/or kenjutsu were practised almost exclusively by the *bushi*, known more commonly today as the *samurai*. Today, people of all walks of life, gender, abilities and cultures can be found practising the art of kendo. No longer is it just confined to the boundary of

Kendo should not be seen as a sport but as a lifetime's study.

Kendo was derived from the art of Japanese samurai *swordsmanship.*

Japan, as it opens its doors to many other countries world-wide. It can also be said that kendo, like other martial arts, is a unifying activity, creating a sense of harmony through its competitive element. This was witnessed in March 1997 when the Heian shrine in Kyoto opened its doors to representatives from around the world to demonstrate the art of iaido, another martial art. At the same time, teams from many different countries took part in the tenth World Kendo Competition.

As with iaido, the philosophy of kendo is challenging. In many ways, it is viewed as contradictory by those who do not appreciate the importance of abandoning their own desires. This is not easy in a competitive world, with its increasingly materialist attitude, but as Musashi Miyamoto, one of Japan's most famous swordsmen (1584–1645), once said: "to win the battle is to be prepared to die."

This is very much the philosophy of the *kendoka*. Practitioners who enter into a fight, primarily concerned with not being hit, will find that their adversaries will more easily score points or win the battle. In kendo, the strike is viewed as a by-product of what has come before and what is

THE CONCEPT OF KENDO

The following is an extract from the All Japan Kendo Federation, highlighting the true concept of kendo and the purpose of practising this art:

- **To mould the mind and body**
- **To cultivate a vigorous spirit**

Through correct and rigid training:
- **To strive for the improvement in the art of kendo**
- **To hold in esteem human courtesy and honour**
- **To associate with others with sincerity**
- **To pursue forever the cultivation of oneself**

Thus, you will be able:
- **To love your country and society**
- **To contribute to the development of culture**
- **To promote peace and prosperity among all peoples**

about to follow, and there is a strong emphasis placed on initiative and taking control (*seme*). This plays an important part in kendo development, along with a constant sense of readiness and alertness (*zanshin*).

The aim of kendo is for *kendoka* to react intuitively, with fluency and elegance. Speed and body movement are of the utmost importance in the delivery of a skilful technique. Yet the aim is not to be the first one to score a point or to win in the kendo practice, but to work together, striving towards good technique, giving and taking along the way. Only in competition should this philosophical aim be different.

On first learning kendo, or any other martial art, it is very important to tread slowly. It is very easy when people wear armour to suddenly feel they can dive in regardless, without appreciating the need for continual practice to develop the skills to a standard acceptable in the art. It is important not only to demonstrate proficiency in the art but to ensure safe practice, both for yourself and your partner.

Kendo places great emphasis on moral values, discipline and self-control. Try to think of kendo not as a sport that you might participate in for a few years, but as a lifetime's study. Mental and physical control are of the utmost importance, since the balance of the two leads to harmony, not only in the art itself, but in your general well-being. It is for this reason that there are four deep-rooted mental hurdles that *kendoka* must overcome: fear, doubt, surprise and confusion. Collectively, these are known as "the four poisons of kendo".

Competition (*shiai*)

When experienced practitioners come together, especially in competition (*shiai*), the atmosphere can be very exciting. Competition is a vital part of kendo, since it provides an opportunity for practitioners to try out, under conditions of pressure and stress, the various techniques. The judges look for good posture, composure and the ability to deliver a strike effectively with all the skill and mental confidence that is required to show a good *kendoka*.

In an effort to avoid kendo competition becoming a violent, attacking activity (sometimes referred to as "bash and dash") based solely on winning, it is important that *kendoka*, especially beginners, develop the mental confidence to remain calm (*shiai geiko*). *Kendoka* strive to remain calm, alert and decisive, and to accept defeat as a guide to developing their technique and skill for the future. A kendo *shiai* usually lasts for five minutes, and the winner is the first to score two points, or a single point if the time limit elapses first. There are three court referees and a senior referee off court. There is also a timekeeper to ensure that the competitors are within the allocated match period. The rules of the competition are always strictly adhered to.

More than 5,000 Japanese boys and girls during the All Japan Children's Military Arts Summer Training Meeting held in Tokyo.

Kendoka *demonstrating the dynamics of the fast cutting action and fighting spirit.*

Scoring in kendo

During the *shiai* there are many opportunities for *kendoka* to learn and refine their skills. For example, there are differences between *shiai* (contests) and *dojo jigeiko* (free practice). This is perhaps best demonstrated in the example of opponents fighting within the parameters of the rules set by the leading organizations. This will result in a winner and a loser and, in comparison to Olympic fencing, where a point is scored simply by making contact with the target, in kendo several elements are required in order for the essential winning point to be scored. These include:

• Creating an opportunity to attack a vulnerable point on the body.

• The accuracy and skill of the strike itself, which must be delivered with the correct spirit – sword and body working together as one.

A very important part of kendo training is *zanshin*, which translates as "good awareness" – that is, of the opponent and the continuing element of battle. It is the ability to take in the environment, being sensitive to any threat or other factors that could lead to injury, even death. *Zanshin* enables *kendoka* to attain a heightened ability and awareness, and thus to react instantaneously to minimize risk.

BENEFITS OF KENDO

The benefits derived from learning kendo affect many aspects of your everyday life. These include:

• **Speed and agility**
• **General fitness**
• **Self-discipline and a positive attitude**
• **Precision and timing**
• **Self-confidence**
• **Self-control and well-being**
• **Comradeship**
• **Inner peace and calm**

clothing *and* equipment

Kendo developed and evolved from actual battlefield conditions and therefore the utilization of armour became essential and intrinsic to the practitioners of this art. As a full contact art, the relevant parts of the body must be well protected. For example, the head guard (*men*) is of extremely durable quality and can withstand the constant strikes made with the *shinai*. There is a set procedure for putting the armour on and great pride is taken to ensure that this is well-maintained, clean and correctly laid out before every training session. Practitioners practise sword exercises prior to any kendo training session, to maintain not only the tradition, but also agility and stamina.

*Practitioner (*kendoka*) sitting (*seiza*) in preparation to place the head armour (*men*), gloves (*kote*) and* shinai *in the correct position, before commencement of practice.*

The kendoka *prepared, fully armoured, bowing (*rei*) to either the* dojo, *instructor or opponent. Note the* shinai *is in a lowered and relaxed position.*

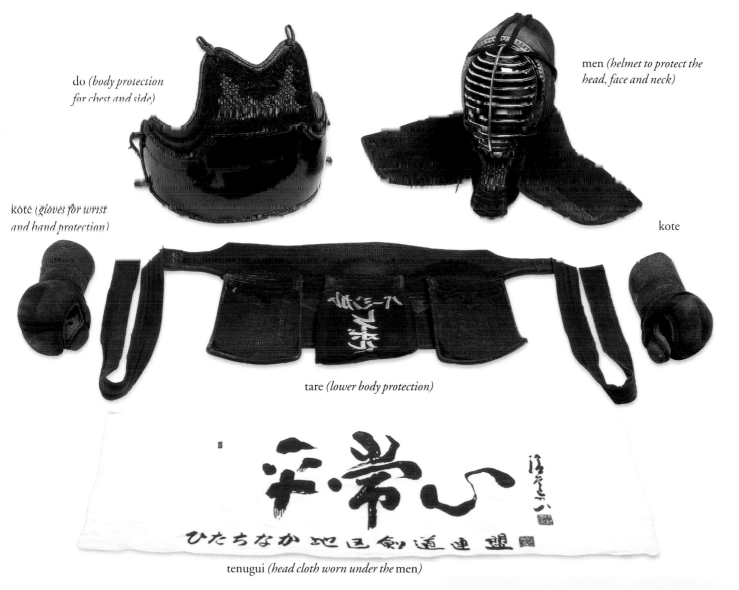

do (*body protection for chest and side*)

men (*helmet to protect the head, face and neck*)

kote (*gloves for wrist and hand protection*)

kote

tare (*lower body protection*)

tenugui (*head cloth worn under the* men)

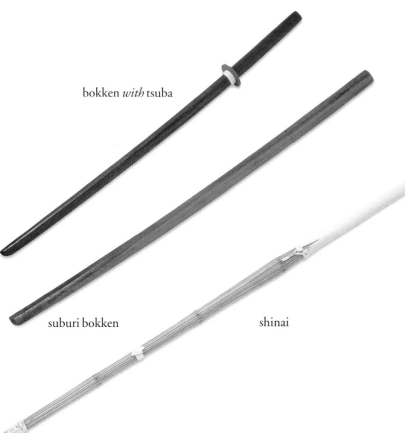

bokken *with* tsuba

suburi bokken

shinai

SAFE PRACTICE AND *DOJO* ETIQUETTE

- It is important that you do not touch a practitioner's armour or *shinai* (bamboo sword), *bokken* (wooden sword) or sword, without that person's permission. It is very important that you not only respect your own clothing and equipment, but also that of fellow practitioners.
- Always treat your *shinai* with respect. Never lean on it when being given instruction or discard it in the *dojo* without respect. Treat your *shinai* as a sword, since this is what it truly represents.
- Never step over a fellow practitioner's *shinai* or armour when it is laid out, whether it is in the *dojo* ready for practice or at the side of the *dojo* in preparation.
- If your armour comes loose, or any of your clothing slips and you need to retie it, move to the side of the *dojo* opposite the *kamiza* (known as the *shimoza*). Go into a kneeling posture (*seiza*) and then readjust your clothing and armour. Never, under any circumstance, adjust, retie or reposition your armour or clothing while standing as this is viewed as disrespectful and puts you at risk of attack in a real battle situation.

Etiquette

Dojo etiquette is very important in kendo. It is aimed at teaching *kendoka* (practitioners) respect for the *dojo* (training environment), their opponents and themselves. While *dojo* etiquette may vary slightly from one kendo club to another, around the world, the following is considered as standard.

SAFETY IN THE *DOJO*

- As you enter the *dojo* perform a bow (*rei*) to the *kamiza* – the area designated as the shrine or that is considered to be the point at which respect is given.
- You should always acknowledge the instructor (*sensei*) with a bow, or some other form that is considered appropriate, as he or she enters the *dojo* or gives you instruction or advice.
- Always be punctual and try to arrive early for training. This demonstrates discipline, respect and dedication.
- Remove your shoes when entering the *dojo*. Not only does this show respect for your training area, it is also hygienic. The Japanese don't usually wear outdoor footwear inside.
- Never drink, smoke or eat in the *dojo*.
- Ensure you are smartly dressed and that your clothing (*keikogi* and *hakama*) are well-pressed and clean. This demonstrates self-discipline and respect for the art.
- As a sign of respect and politeness, always pass behind any practitioner wearing armour. This shows respect and ensures safety in the *dojo*. If, however, you have to pass in front of an armoured practitioner who is seated, pause, make a slight *rei*, and extend your hand as you pass.
- If "*yame*" is called, you must immediately halt whatever you are doing. *Yame* is Japanese for "stop" and this rule applies to general practice, basics and competition.
- During all training, great emphasis is placed on manners (*reigi*) and respect. As with any sport or discipline, there is always a potential for injury, and so it is very important that you maintain self-control and a respectful attitude towards everybody within the *dojo*.

THE BOW

1 ◁ Kneel down with your hands placed on your thighs. Keep your back straight and look to the front. This position is called *seiza*. Place your armour neatly at your right side with the guard (*tsuba*) on the sword handle level with your left knee. You should keep a relaxed yet assertive posture.

2 ◁ As you lower your body forwards, place the palm of your left hand, then right hand, flat on the floor, making a diamond shape, with your forefingers and thumbs touching. Keep your elbows tucked in and perform the bow (*rei*) as a sign of respect to the *dojo*, instructor and the practice that is about to commence. This *rei* is also performed to the spirit of kendo (*kamiza*), usually towards the practitioner's right side.

MEDITATION (*MOKUSO*)

This is a period of concentration, performed while kneeling, and is the position used at the beginning and end of both kendo and iaido training. It is important to rid yourself of any worries, concerns and distractions, and it is considered helpful to think of running water (*rishu*) as an aid. The nature of flowing water represents tranquillity – one drop may be meaningless in the context of many thousands, yet each drop in itself is part of an important element of nature.

◁ Bring your hands together, palms upward, in a cupped position. Close your eyes and breathe in slowly through your nose. Imagine the breath going up over your head and down into the pit of your stomach. Breathe out slowly through your mouth. The duration of this exercise varies, depending on your experience and your teacher's (*sensei's*) instruction.

Exercise | Warm-up

Practitioners perform a variety of warm-up exercises before putting on their armour. Great emphasis is placed on maintaining a high mental focus on the technical purity of the art. At the start of training, practitioners practise what is known as *keiko* (free practice). Further warm-up is performed, when wearing armour, at the start of training.

WARM-UP 1 – *Loosening your leg muscles and feet.*

△ Step forwards with your right leg and place your hands on your hips. Keep your rear leg straight and apply a forwards and downwards pushing pressure. Change to your left leg forwards and repeat the exercise 2 to 3 times each side.

WARM-UP 3 – *Stretching of legs, hips and upper body in order to increase mobility.*

△ Stand with your legs fairly wide apart and drop your hands so that your fingertips touch the floor. Repeat 3 to 4 times.

WARM-UP 2 *Stretching the sides of your body for flexibility.*

△ Bring your right arm up and over your head and place your left hand on your hip. Keep your feet facing forwards as you stretch your arm over your head, as if trying to touch the floor with your fingers. Keep your body relaxed for maximum benefit. Change to your left arm and repeat the exercise 2 to 3 times each side.

WARM-UP 4 – *An exercise to help stretch your body, with particular emphasis on leg muscles and controlled breathing.*

△ Keeping the same stance as in the previous exercise, take your right hand across to touch your left foot. Repeat on the opposite side, using your left hand to touch your right foot. Repeat the exercise 3 to 4 times each side.

Prior to any exercise using the *shinai*, perform a bow (*rei*) as a sign of respect to the art and your fellow practitioners. The *shinai* is made of four pieces of bamboo, which are bound together for lightness and strength. The following show the preparation needed prior to starting the basic cutting exercises and techniques.

SUBURI

Basic cutting exercises, known as *suburi*, are performed by the practitioner as part of basic practice, both prior to wearing armour and with full armour. The practice is also performed individually, in a group session or with a partner. The exercises are to develop technique, build strength, speed and stamina, with the additional benefit of developing focus, concentration and correct breathing. A shout, known as *kiai*, is made on the completion of each strike.

PREPARATION

❶ △ Stand in a formal position, with your feet facing forwards, back straight and chin up. Hold the *shinai* in a relaxed position in your left hand.

❷ △ Lower your body about 30 degrees to perform a bow (*rei*). This is performed to your instructor and also when opposite a partner before commencement of practice.

❸ △ Bring the *shinai* up to your left hip in preparation to move three paces forwards.

❹ △ Draw your *shinai* as you step forwards and go down into a squatting position (*sonkyo*). Keep your heels together with your feet facing outwards at a 45-degree angle. The *kendoka* (practitioner) on the left is demonstrating the angle of the draw, while the one on the right is in the *sonkyo* position.

EXERCISE – *Following the preparation, various exercises can be performed using the* shinai.

❺ △ This is the standing position (*kamae*). The *kendoka* on the left is demonstrating the angle of the *shinai* in the forwards position. The *kendoka* on the right demonstrates the side view.

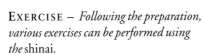

❶ ◁ Place the *shinai* in the small of your back, just behind your hips, and rotate your hips and the *shinai* in a circular motion towards the right.

❷ ▷ Rotate the *shinai* in a circular motion towards your left side. Repeat several times.

Preparation | Wearing of armour

Before wearing the head guard (*men*), you must first put on a cotton cloth called a *tenugui*. This cloth serves three purposes: it soaks up perspiration to prevent it running into your eyes; it keeps your hair out of your face and eyes; and it acts as a cushion under the head guard. The *tenugui* usually displays *dojo* or country information.

FITTING THE HEAD GUARD (MEN)

1 △ Lay the *men* (head guard) to your right side on top of the *kote* (hand guard), making sure the *tenugui* is placed on top of your *men*. Your *shinai* must be placed to your left side with the *tsuba* in line with your left knee.

2 △ Lift the *tenugui* and stretch it out in front of your body.

3 △ Wrap the *tenugui* around your head. The *kendoka* on the left is demonstrating the position of the *tenugui* and ties, while the one on the right is showing how to tie the *tenugui* above the forehead.

4 ◁ The *tenugui* is now correctly tied in preparation for the *men*.

5 ▷ Secure the *men* by taking the cords or strings (*himo*) and wrapping them around your head. The *kendoka* on the left is showing the *himo* being pulled and wrapped around the *men*. The *kendoka* on the right, in profile, is showing the finishing position of the *himo*, neatly in place.

6 △ Next, the hand guards (*kote*) are put on – first the left and then the right hand. This ensures that the right hand is free for as long as possible, should it be necessary to defend against an attack. The *kendokas* are now ready to commence practice.

7 ▷ A standing bow (*rei*) is performed as a sign of respect to your training partner.

8 △ Lower your body into the squatting (*sonkyo*) position, balancing on the balls of your feet (heels touching) and with your knees at about 45 degrees. This is the start position of all practice in kendo, including basics, grading and competition. Hold the *shinai* out from the centre of your body, with your right hand gripping the handle (*tsuka*), above the left hand. Your partner squats opposite so that the tips of your *shinai* are just touching.

Technique | Basic competition (*shiai*)

△ A standing bow (*rei*) is performed as a sign of respect to your partner.

GOOD POSTURE

A vital part of being skilled in kendo is maintaining a well-balanced and upright posture. Whether you are moving forwards or backwards, correct body posture is an important part of delivering a strike that has the correct force and energy. Leaning to the side usually results in an ineffective strike leaving you vulnerable to attack.

STANCE

Your stance is an extremely important part of kendo practice. When standing normally, your feet should be a shoulder-width apart. Move forwards with your right foot, so that the heel is in line with the toes of your left foot. The heel of your left foot should be slightly raised – but no more than 1 in (2.5 cm), allowing you to move with agility and speed.

At the beginning of each basic competition (*shiai*) session, two contestants step into the contest area (*shiajo*) and bow to each other as a sign of respect. They then advance to the centre of the court, before drawing their shinai and sinking down into the squatting position (*sonkyo*). The main referee will shout "*hajime*" ("begin"), at which point the contestants stand and usually let out a shout, known as *kiai*, before initiating an attack. It is often thought that this relates to the philosophy of shouting as a way of generating fear within the opponent. Shouting is also thought to produce extra strength for the attack. The two contestants then try to score points by striking specific parts of the body: the head (*men*), the throat (*tsuki*), the sides of the body (*do*) or the wrist (*kote*). Even where a point is scored, contestants continue to maintain fighting spirit until the senior court judge yells "*yame*" (stop).

The contestants then reposition themselves at the centre of the court and the contest continues, until either one has scored the match point to win the *shiai*. At the end, both contestants lower themselves into the *sonkyo* position. As there is no *saya* (scabbard that protects the sword), the *shinai* is not sheathed but is placed in a natural position to the left side of the body (similar to wearing a sword). This is performed prior to and at the end of the competition. The contestants then walk away backwards, bow to each, turn and exit.

HAND POSITION
Your left hand should be as near to the base of the hilt of the handle of the *shinai* (bamboo sword) as possible, with your right hand just below the *tsuba* (the guard that divides the handle from the "blade"). A firm yet relaxed grip on the *shinai* is required – it is the third and fourth fingers of your hands that actually grasp the sword, while the rest of your hands, wrists, forearms and shoulders should be relaxed. Holding the *shinai* in a hard and aggressive way burns up unnecessary energy, leading to fatigue and an ineffective style. This hand position does not change throughout the practice, whether you are holding the *shinai* with or without gloves (*kote*). Once you have the correct grip, make sure that the hilt of the *shinai* is approximately one to two hand grips away from your lower abdomen. Don't rest the *shinai* against your body, since this is considered disrespectful.

Striking techniques in kendo are mainly aimed at three areas of the body, namely the head (*men*), (centre, left and right) body (*do*) wrist (*kote*), with thrust or lunge (*tsuki*). These areas are well-protected with armour, but were vulnerable in the days of the *samurai*. Some striking terms have the same name as each area's protective equipment.

SHOMEN UCHI – MEN STRIKE

◁ *Shomen uchi* is a cut executed towards the top of the head (*men*).

△ Aim to strike the centre of the head with the end of the *shinai*.

▽ Evading a *shomen uchi* strike to the top of the head and preparing to counter-attack.

▽ Counter-attack with *do waza* (body out). The aim is to cut the side of the body as the aggressor moves through to strike and presents a vulnerable position. This requires precision of timing and accuracy.

KOTE

▽ This strike is known as cutting the wrist (*kote*), in which the *shinai* makes contact with the forearm anywhere between the wrist and about half way to the elbow. It is a strike coming from above, and cuts are permitted to the front of the arm if your opponent's *shinai* is in a low position, and to the left arm when it is raised, depending on whether your opponent is moving forwards or backwards.

CHUDAN TSUKI

△ A thrusting action to your opponent's throat. This is performed, especially in competition, to try and score a point. The partner is well-protected by a firm padded guard which covers the throat area.

DO

◁ This is a cut to the side of the body between the armpit and the hip bone. It can be performed from either side and is a diagonal cut from above.

△ Upon making contact with the armour, the practitioner making the strike will shout "*do*", as this is the part of the body they are striking.

KATATA (THRUST)

▽ A single-handed thrust to your opponent's throat is known as *katata tsuki. Caution: this technique can be very dangerous, which is why kendo armour has protective padding, extending from the face grid to the breast bone. It is important that this part of the armour, in particular, is well-maintained, but even so, accidents have been known to happen, when the shinai has accidentally penetrated underneath the padding. Take great care that your armour is of good quality and is correctly fitted.*

△ In this close-up of the correct footwork, note the short stance, with the feet a shoulder-width apart, the weight on the balls of your feet and the rear heel slightly raised. This is the main stance adopted by all practitioners.

MEN UCHI

▽ The movement through to strike the head (*men*) is used in various exercises. For example, *keiko* (free practice), which is divided into various areas including *uchikomi keiko* and *keri kaishi*, during which students rapidly attack exposed target areas of their opponent with power and full concentration.

TSUBA ZERIAI

▽ *Tsuba zeriai* is the name given to this position, in which you and your opponent are very close together, with both *shinai* pushing against each other, looking for an opening from which to strike.

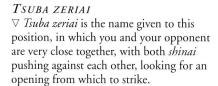

JIGEIKO

When practitioners have been through the various exercises, they get the opportunity to put their training into practice against each other, in what is known as *jigeiko*. This is not a free-for-all session, but a time to develop their skill, timing and precision, and to fine-tune their techniques. This is a form of practice in kendo and is not specific to competition or grading.

IAIDO

Iaido is the art of drawing your sword and striking an armed opponent at lightning speed. It is the art of strategy, achieving precision in all aspects of mental and physical ability, including accurate footwork, balanced posture and critical timing. "Live" blades are razor-sharp and experienced practitioners are the only ones permitted to use them. The risk involved is thought worthwhile, because this is the only way to achieve the ultimate in awareness and concentration, and to bring mind and body together in total harmony.

IAIDO

history *and*
philosophy

Iaido derives from the ancient way of the *samurai* warrior (*bushi*), and the forerunner of the art we know today, *iai-jutsu*, was used in earnest on the battlefield, whereas iaido was designed to practise "the way of the sword".

Evidence suggests that the *bokken* used today in iaido has been used as a weapon since about AD 400. The *bokken* is a solid wooden stick with the same shape, weight and approximate length as a sword, and is usually made of red or white oak. *Bokken* technique was followed by the art of *tachikaki* (drawing the sword from its scabbard). The blade (*tachi* or *katana*), was long and straight and the Japanese warrior would carry it on his left side. A shorter blade was used for quick-draw techniques, known as *batto*.

The curved swords seen today are not the original Japanese swords. Indeed, they were flat, straight swords of primitive construction, used for simple strikes and thrusts. It was around AD 940, the middle of the Heian period, that the single-edged, slightly curved sword appeared, and the superb skill of the Japanese warrior developed. Until that time, single-handed swords were used in battle by mounted warriors. They were protected by heavy armour, using the right hand to draw and cut the enemy.

Sometime during the mid-16th century, battle strategy changed and mounted warriors replaced foot warriors who wore lighter armour and used techniques requiring both hands on the sword hilt.

Dominance of the *bushi*

In 1189, the *samurai bushi* of the Minamoto clan finally gained complete military and political dominance in Japan, a position they maintained for nearly 700 years, until 1868. In the early part of the 14th century, however, there was a

Haruna Matsuo Sensei – 7th- dan *iaido.*

Practitioners from all over the world practising iaido at the Heian Shrine, Japan.

decline in the military skills of the *bushi*, but this was recti-fied during the third Ashikaga Shogun Yoshimitsu period (1358–1508), when encouragement was given to proper training in such skills as archery, swordsmanship and the use of *naginata*, a curved blade spear.

The ability to draw the blade in a bold, fast and dynamic upward, sweeping movement, was intrinsic to the *bushi*. Nevertheless, this was not a standardized style of fighting, and it was during the early Heian period that much of Japanese culture was imported from China. It was not only the Chinese martial arts that captured the imagination and interest of the Japanese, it was also the study of Chinese philosophy, painting and poetry.

What is iaido?

Although iaido may be classed as a separate martial art, it is closely related and complementary to kendo. Kendo practice requires two people fencing each other armed with *shinai* (bamboo swords) and wearing armour, whereas iaido is prac-tised on an individual basis wearing a *gi* , *juban*, *hakama* and *obi*. Practitioners use a real or an imitation sword, called an *iaito*. The aim of the exercise is to perform a set series of

movements (*kata*), in which the sword is drawn, an imagi-nary opponent is cut, and then the sword is resheathed. The ultimate purpose of iaido, however, is to master the ability to overcome your enemy without the sword being drawn in the first place – in other words, to conquer your opponent "spir-itually", with the sword still in the sheath, and so resolve problems without having to even resort to violence. There is one quote that explains this way of thinking: "Your mind is not disturbed by you being beaten up, but by you beating up others."

It has been said that many iaido moves passed down over the centuries were secret techniques related to Zen practice and enlightenment, as well as the secret physical techniques (*waza*). In the 15th century, a Zen master, Takuan, discussed with Yagyu Munenori, a sword master, the concept of the "unfettered mind". This was defined as a person who could remain calm in the face of adversity. They agreed on the word *fudoshin* to encapsulate this concept. The term came to describe any person who demonstrates clarity of mind and purpose, even in the most difficult situations.

There are various traditional styles of iaido still practised in Japan today, although many have been lost over the

The true spirit of martial arts is founded upon detail and correctness. Note the positioning of the feet, whereby further movement is easily effected.

centuries. Those that have survived have been passed down from generation to generation. These include muso jikiden ryu, muso shinden ryu and katori shinto ryu. These styles of iaido are based on the more traditional schools of swordsmanship, employing fast-drawing techniques.

It is widely believed that Hayashizaki Jinnosuke Shigenobu founded the school of iai jutsu (the precursor of iaido) in 1560. His sword techniques were perfected by Eishin in the 18th century, since which time the muso jikiden ryu style has developed, as well as the eishin ryu forms.

In 1968-69, a system known as seitei gata iaido was developed, in order to provide a basic system around which all the varied styles of iaido could be unified.

Competition (*taikai*)

Seitei gata iaido forms an important basis for gradings in iaido, no matter how senior or junior the grade. Many practitioners take part in competitions (*taikai*) throughout the year, and while there is an element of practitioners being able to demonstrate their own style, it is vitally important that

Assisting practitioners to develop their skills in iaido.

Two Japanese swordsmen illustrate the concept of zanshin *– total mental alertness and awareness.*

The meeting of blades.

they demonstrate the basic seitei gata iaido, so that the judges can truly evaluate their skills and techniques.

Taikai, in iaido, is performed by two practitioners running through their routines at the same time. Individual performance is judged by three referees who are looking and judging on a wide variety of technical, physical and mental attributes.

Many of the basic rules for the art of kendo also apply to iaido competition, with the addition of *kokorogamae*, which means "mental posture". *Kokorogamae* includes calmness, vision (*metsuke*), spirit, concentration, distance (between individuals) and timing. The Japanese expression of *shin gi tai-no-ichi* (meaning "heart, technique and body as one") sums up the aims of *kokorogamae* perfectly.

BENEFITS OF IAIDO

The benefits derived from iaido affect many aspects of your everyday life. These include:

- Speed and agility
- Fitness
- Self-discipline and a positive attitude
- Precision and timing
- Self-confidence
- Self-control and well-being
- Comradeship
- Inner peace and calm
- Harmony of mind and body

clothing *and* equipment

The colour of the *hakama* in iaido can range from white, black and blue, to pin stripe grey or other similar colours. The materials of the clothing also vary from the less expensive polyester and cotton fabric to silk. Practitioners usually wear a *zekken*, which is a chest patch embroidered with their name, *dojo* and nationality. Great pride is taken in appearance, ensuring that all clothing fits correctly. *Bokken* and swords should be well cared for, being cleaned and maintained regularly, after every practice. It is equally important to check *bokken* and swords prior to the commencement of practice, to ensure safety in the *dojo* environment.

Blue jacket The jackets are available in a variety of colours and material, black, white and blue are the most common colours worn.

Hakama A folded skirt, similar to culottes. There are five pleats at the front and one at the rear. Wearing a good-quality *hakama* is recommended, since it is extremely durable and will maintain its shape throughout practice.

Obi The long, wide, band that is wrapped around the body underneath the *hakama*.

Zori The sandals that are used mainly outside the *dojo*. They are designed to be slipped on to either bare feet or over the *tabi*. Never wear *zori* inside the *dojo* or when training as this is seen as both disrespectful and dangerous.

Tabi These are the formal footwear that are allowed in the *dojo*. They are usually of cotton material with a non-slip base.

Shinken The *shinken* is a "live" blade – razor-sharp and made in the traditional Japanese way, by folding the metal many times to obtain a blade that is light, yet incredibly strong. *Shinken* is expensive to buy, whether you purchase an original or a new blade.

Iaito The *iaito* is another type of practice sword used in iaido, which has a stainless-steel replica of a live blade (*shinken*).

Sageo The cord that is secured to the scabbard. The small wooden piece through which the *sageo* is fed is known as the *kurigata*.

Bokken Most people start iaido practice using either a *bokken* or an *iaito*. A *bokken* is a wooden replica sword, usually made of white or red oak, with the same shape (curvature) as a real sword and a plastic guard (*tsuba*). The disadvantage of using a *bokken* is that there is no *saya* (the sheath, or scabbard, that covers the blade). This means that the practitioner will not benefit from *saya* practice with the left hand, which is equally as important as the right hand in the art of iaido.

Tsuba The *tsuba* is the circular fitting which is placed between the handle (*tsuka*) and sword. On a *bokken* it is usually made of plastic and on a live blade can be a decorative piece of craftsmanship.

Zekken The embroidered patch with the practitioner's name, *dojo* and nationality written in Japanese.

Cleaning kit This includes *uchiko* powder, which is used to remove acidity and grime from the blade, caused through contact with the hand during practice. The powder ball is gently tapped on both sides of the blade, from base to tip, to cover it with powder.

Etiquette

Dojo etiquette is very important in iaido, not only as a sign of respect to the art, training area and fellow practitioners, but also to ensure everybody's safety. Etiquette is quite involved, as it follows Japanese tradition in placing great emphasis on the smallest detail. Using any weapon is dangerous if not handled with utmost respect.

1 △ Before walking on to the training area, hold your sword in your left hand with the blade (*hi*) facing upwards. When you arrive at your position for training, raise the sword to just below your waist (*taito*).

2 △ At this point, your sword hand is resting just above your left hip bone, with the sword angled slightly inwards at about 45 degrees.

△ Side view showing correct posture and angle of the sword.

3 △ Turn towards the *kamiza*, the area designated as the place of respect. This is usually, but not necessarily, towards the east of the *dojo*. You now pass the sword over to your right hand.

4 △ Turn the sword as you pass it from your left to your right hand, so that the edge of the blade is facing down towards the floor.

5 △ Bring the sword down and hold it at a 30-degree angle on the right of your body, with the edge of the blade facing downwards.

6 △ Bow to *kamiza*, ensuring minimum sword movement. This is a small bow only, so lower your upper body by no more than 15 degrees. Lower your eyes naturally as you bow. There is no need to keep looking forward, as you are bowing to the art, not an opponent.

7 △ Return to the upright position. Pass the sword back to your left hand. Make sure your thumb is looped around the cord (*sageo*).

8 △ Position the sword back on your left hip.

9 △ Lower your body into the kneeling position (*seiza*), keeping your eyes forward (*metsuke*) on your opponent. To prevent the *hakama* becoming entangled with your legs and feet, perform a V-shaped cutting action with the knife edge of your right hand, known as *hakama sabaki*.

10 △ Place your left knee down on the floor first, followed by your right knee.

11 △ Lower your body and settle on your heels. Rest the sword lightly on your left thigh and place your right hand near the top of your right thigh. Ideally, your hand should be just under the guard (*tsuka*), for ease of drawing the blade.

12 △ Pass the sword from your left hand to your right.

13 △ Holding the *sageo* with your left fingers, slide your left hand down the sword. Stop approximately 4 in (10 cm) before you reach the end of the scabbard (*saya*).

14 △ Hold the sword in front of your body as you pass the *sageo* underneath the sword with the fingers of your left hand.

15 △ Place the sword neatly on the floor, directly in front of you. Avoid making any unnecessary movements.

16 △ Next, place your left hand, then your right, on to your upper thighs.

17 △ Lower your body, placing your left hand on the floor, followed by your right, with thumbs and forefingers forming a diamond shape. With elbows tucked in, keep the back of your head in line with your spine as you perform the bow (*rei*).

18 ▷ Following the bow, revert to an upright kneeling posture. Take hold of the sword with both hands, with the palm of your right hand facing upwards and the left facing downwards. As you bring the sword back towards you, place your left thumb down the centre of your *hakama* to make an opening for the sword. Gently push the end of the scabbard (*saya*), known as the *kojiri*, through the ties of the hakama and *obi*, towards your left side, so that the sword sits comfortably, ready to commence practice.

19 △ Bring the *sageo* over the back of the *saya*, underneath and to the front. Tie the *sageo* through the *hakama* ties (*himo*). The tie is either a single loop pushed up between the ties, or a double loop (which is one loop inside another).

Exercise | Warm-up

Warm-up exercises include the use of the sword and general body movements similar to other arts. Primarily the emphasis is on the sword warm-up moves, to work the relevant parts of the body prior to technical practice, and using either a *bokken* (wooden replica) or *shinken* (live blade), depending upon level of qualification.

WARM-UP 1 – *This vertical cutting technique is known as* kirioroshi.

1 △ Draw your sword into the centre ready position (*chudan kamae*). Keep an upright posture with shoulders relaxed, back straight and the heel of your rear foot slightly raised. Your right hand is near the sword's guard (*tsuba*) and your left hand is towards the end of the handle (*kashira*). Make sure the V shape of your hand is uppermost on the *kashira*, with your thumb and forefinger on either side.

2 △ Ensuring your grip is secure yet relaxed, raise the sword above your head (*jodan kamae*), ensuring that the tip of the blade remains horizontal. When cutting, avoid a hard grip, since this burns up unnecessary energy, which thus restricts your technique.

3 △ Step forwards as you start to extend your arms fully in a "reaching" action, and commence a large, circular cut. The technique finishes with the sword at your waistline. Make sure you are looking straight ahead, maintaining the same body posture.

4 △ Once the sword has completed its cutting action, the tip of the blade (*kissaki*) should be in line with the *habaki* – the metal fixture about 1 in (2.5 cm) long seated on the blade next to the *tsuba* between the handle (*tsuka*) and sword.

WARM-UP 2 – *The horizontal cutting technique is called* nukitsuke.

1 ◁ With the sword in your right hand, held across your body, the blade should be level with your upper left arm with the tip pointing backwards. Using a large, circular action across your body, swing the sword back towards your right shoulder. The tip of the blade should be approximately in line with your right nipple. *Note: this cut is usually performed against an opponent in a sitting position, aiming for the eyes. When performed against a standing opponent, the target area is either the chest or abdomen.*

2 ▷ Cut in a circular action. Your left hand plays an important part in all sword techniques, as it assists with the drawing of the blade. Make sure the left hand pulls the *saya* round the small of the back in a horizontal action. This action is simultaneous with the drawing action. The tip of the blade is level with the right side of the chest, at about nipple height.

Technique | First level

The following is a selection of techniques taken from particular styles known as *muso jiki-den ryu*, *eishin ryu*, and *oku-iai*. Once familiar and competent with *seitei gata iaido*, practitioners move on to practise the other *kata* within their chosen style. The intention is to develop not only the skill of drawing and cutting, but also the strategy behind the form.

TSUKI KAGE

YAE GAKI

TSUKE KOMI

△ *Tsuki kage* is a *kata* designed to enable the practitioner to draw and cut from a side attack. The aim is to draw the sword from a low posture, moving underneath the opponent's arms as the opponent attempts a cut to the head. This is an upward cut to both wrists. A variation is to cut just the right or left wrist.

△ The first technique is taken out of a form (*kata*) called *yae gaki*. You perform this technique towards the end of the *kata*, when your opponent is on the floor and is making a final cutting action at the lower part of your leg. To prevent the cut, use the side of your sword (*shinogi*) in a blocking technique, before preparing to make the final cut.

△ This move is taken from the last part of the *kata* known as *tsuke komi*. It demonstrates the "blood wipe" action following the final cut, which is one way of cleaning the blade before sheathing (*noto*).

OROSHI

△ *Oroshi* is a cut made to the side of your opponent's neck.

SEITEI GATA IAIDO

Today, many practitioners of iaido practise *seitei gata iaido*. This comprises a set of basic forms (*katas*) used in most styles of iaido to encourage uniformity in practice, so that people can be graded to a common standard. This, however, does not exclude the classical styles that are a part of iaido. Iaido is about strategy, and many of the forms demonstrate the importance of interpretation, timing, positioning, skill, vision and other qualities needed to survive in the day of the *samurai*. Today, these qualities are essential to the development of good character.

FORMS (*KATA*)
Performed from a sitting (*seiza*) position

Number	Name	Meaning
Ippon me (1)	*Mae*	Front
Nihon me (2)	*Ushiro*	Rear
Sanbon me (3)	*Uke nagashi*	Catch and slide off
Yonhon me (4)	*Tsuka ate*	Strike with the *tsuka* (handle)

Performed from a standing posture

Gohon me (5)	*Kesa giri*	Cross cut
Roppon me (6)	*Morote tsuki*	Thrust with both hands
Nanahon me (7)	*Sanpo giri*	Cut in three directions
Hachihon me (8)	*Gan men ate*	Strike to centre of face
Kyubon me (9)	*Soe te tsuki*	Thrust with supporting hand
Juppon me (10)	*Shiho giri*	Four-direction cut

Technique | Advanced level

The following shows a selection of techniques taken from a *kata* performed in the *muso jikiden eishin ryu* style. The first two pictures demonstrate one of the cuts in *iwanami*, which means "waterfall", followed by a sequence of moves taken from *taki-otoshi* against a rear attack.

TATE HIZA – Start position.

△ This position is called *tate hiza*, meaning "standing knee". The *samurai* used to sit in this fashion, since when they were wearing armour they could not easily sit in the normal sitting (*seiza*) position. The above position involves sitting with your left leg tucked under your body and your right leg slightly forwards and bent at the knee. This is a difficult posture for many Westerners to adopt, especially those with long legs. The Japanese are usually smaller in stature and are more easily able to sit in this position.

Finishing kneeling position.

△ This is the finishing posture at the end of some of the techniques performed in *eishin ryu* and *oku den*. After the cut, place the sword back in the scabbard (*saya*) – this is known as the *noto* movement. Next, bring your right foot back towards the left, maintaining a stable posture.

IWANAMI

❶ △ This is part of the *iwanami kata* where you have turned and drawn your sword to your right side, taking hold of the blade with your left hand.

❷ △ Following the preparation to strike, you thrust the sword upwards and forwards into the stomach region. There are several other moves before this *kata* is complete.

❸ △ Using the *bokken*, we can practise the striking part of this technique to develop the take down which forms part of this *kata*.

❹ △ This demonstrates the *hiki taoshi* movement, in which the opponent is pushed down on to the floor by placing the blade of your sword (*bokken*) on their right shoulder. This requires effective hip and body movement to be successful.

Technique | *Okuden*

Okuiai (or *okuden*) is one of the advanced levels offering a selection of standing and sitting forms using a variety of strategies to defeat the opponent. For example, a *kata* called *shinobu* (stealth – tapping the ground), in a scenario of darkness, encourages the opponent to make the first cut so that you know their position and can defend yourself.

TAKI OTOSHI

❶ △ This is the first part of *taki otoshi*, where the opponent tries to grip the scabbard of your sword. As you feel the grip, the intention is to go with the grab in a sequence of moves, to eventually disengage the opponent.

❷ △ Pushing the sword in a downwards motion weakens the opponent's grip of the sheath (*saya*).

❸ △ Keep the momentum going in an upwards direction to fully disengage the opponent's grip.

SODOME

△ Applying a stalking strategy, the intention is to cut three hidden opponents to the side of the neck, as you move forwards.

RYOZUME – *Restrictive movement against obstacle or wall.*

△ In view of the restriction, the sword is drawn very tightly in a forwards motion. This is followed by a lunge into the opponent.

Technique | *Uke nagashi*

The following pictures and captions are not fully instructional and are intended to show you an outline only of one of the *seitei gata iaido kata*. This *kata* is number three (*sanbon me*) and known as *uke nagashi* (catch and slide off). It demonstrates the strategy of defending against a single opponent to the side, from a kneeling position.

❶ ◁ Turn to your right side and kneel down. Take both hands off your sword and place them on your thighs.

❷ ▷ Look towards your imaginary opponent, who is about 6 ft (2m) away. Your opponent has drawn his sword, which he has positioned at the right side of his head (the technique of the sword being prepared at the right side of the head is known as *hasso kamae*). As he moves forwards, start to draw your sword and bring your left foot forwards, so that it is just in front of your right knee. Raise your sword upwards to deflect the opponent's downwards cut.

❸ △ As you stand, parry the cut by bringing your right foot to your left, as if standing "pigeon-toed". Your toes are not touching. This position ensures you are moving to the side of your opponent, to evade the cut and prepare the counter-attack.

❹ △ Pull your left foot back at about 18 degrees and cut down at a slight angle. Bring your left hand on to your sword as you turn in towards your opponent, and cut downwards at a slight diagonal angle, right to left (from your opponent's left shoulder to right hip).

❺ △ The cut will finish at a horizontal position and it is important to still maintain *metsuke* (direction of gaze – looking at your opponent and the wider environment) and *zanshin* (awareness), keeping alert in the event of any further danger.

6 ◁ Change your hand grip on the sword so that the blade is resting on your right knee.

△ This detail shows the correct hand grip once you have reversed the sword in preparation to returning it to its scabbard (*saya*).

7 ◁ Perform a reverse *noto* (sheathing the sword) by bringing the sword from the right knee, around the front of your body, so that it is positioned at the mouth of the scabbard (*saya*) the open end of the *saya* is known as the *koiguchi*.

△ This is the hand and sword position at the beginning of the *noto*, before sheathing.

8 △ Lower your body, aiming to fully sheath the sword as your keft knee touches the ground. Keep looking (*metsuke*) to where your opponent has fallen, and be alert (*zanshin*) in case there are other opponents. Return to the standing position.

9 ▷ You can practise this particular *uke nagashi kata* with a real opponent, both of you armed with a wooden sword (*bokken*), but careful timing is needed to prevent injury. Working with a partner is useful, because it gives you a real feel for the blocking action, especially the correct angle of the sword, so that your opponent's blade slides off yours when it makes contact.

SHINTO RYU

心道流

Shinto ryu is a street defence strategy encompassing the "hard" (forceful self-defence) and "soft" (acceptance and deflection) elements of various martial arts styles. It has developed into a unique self-defence system suitable for all, irrespective of age, fitness or gender. Shinto ryu teaches practitioners skills they can adapt to any situation: hard techniques might be required in response to aggression or physical violence, yet shinto ryu's softer techniques might be more appropriate in an unsolicited or threatening situation.

SHINTO RYU 心道流

history *and* philosophy

The martial arts that are popular today originated and evolved, sometimes over many hundreds of years, from the concepts and ideas of visionary individuals whose belief systems and cultures moulded and shaped their skills and techniques. Today, new systems and styles continue to develop throughout the world.

Shinto ryu is one of the disciplines practised under the umbrella organization of the European Martial Arts Academy, and its name means "nature's way" or "spirit of nature" – *shinto* meaning "nature" or "shrine" and *ryu* meaning "the way". It is by understanding its name that we gain an insight into how the system works, by developing self-defence skills in a "natural way".

The Junior Defence Line specializes in developing the well-being of children and young people, and works within the European Martial Arts Academy. It offers a basic street defence system for children and young people, to help them feel more confident and capable of protecting themselves in the street and at school. Bullying is a major problem within many societies and most bullies are usually cowards. Yet their victims can be traumatized and scarred for life. The principles of shinto ryu spill into this very important area of developing good attitude, discipline and respect.

Children develop confidence by learning how to defend themselves against an aggressive attack. Physical defence is encouraged as a last resort.

Underlying principles

The philosophy of this discipline never manifests itself in seeking harm. Instead, it strives to equip practitioners with techniques that allow them to walk away from difficult situations. Defusing techniques are of paramount importance, but we need confidence to use these skills effectively.

Emphasis is placed on restraining techniques. Street clothing and footwear are encouraged in some training sessions, to give a feeling of reality.

Having knowledge of the physical skills we can put into practice at times of threat and danger can increase our confidence to handle a particular situation. Our body language gives away a great deal about us – research has identified that many victims of street crimes looked like victims before any aggression occurred, and it is possible to minimize risk by looking more confident. We only have to look at the posture used in many of the martial arts. The upright relaxed posture, with shoulders back and looking forwards, projects a perception of awareness, confidence and strength. As Musashi Miyamoto, one of Japan's most famous swordsmen (1584–1645), once said: "Perception is strong and sight is weak!"

Part of shinto ryu is learning once more to trust our intuition, an attribute that we have become complacent about in today's technological and materialistic society. How many times have you felt uncomfortable about a person you have been introduced to, and sometime later this person does something to harm you in some way? Recalling your initial feelings, you say to yourself, "I knew I could not trust that person", and yet you still allowed that situation to develop, not having the confidence to listen to your gift of intuition.

Shinto ryu in practice

Shinto ryu is a modern discipline. Practical techniques are taught based on a "star" movement, which allows you to defend yourself from any conceivable angle – whether standing or seated. Reality is the key to this system of self-defence. Practitioners are taught how to respond to different real-world situations, such as being threatened on public transport, for example, in cars, at work and many other environments. Shinto ryu also teaches you how to improvize with objects you are likely to have at hand, such as using a chair or small table as a barrier, as part of a self-defence strategy.

The use of a *shinai* (bamboo stick) has also been incorporated, but not in the same way as in the art of kendo. It is used to replicate a potential weapon such as a piece of wood, iron bar or pole that may be at hand, so that the practitioner can learn to strike and defend effectively.

BENEFITS OF SHINTO RYU

The benefits derived from learning shinto ryu affect many aspects of your everyday life. These include:

- Speed and agility
- Fitness and stamina
- Awareness and intuition
- Self-confidence
- Self-control and well-being
- Precision and timing
- Respect and self-discipline
- Comradeship
- Inner peace and calm
- Stress reduction
- Character development

Exercise | Warm-up

The following is a sample of some of the exercises performed in shinto ryu prior to training. Certain advanced exercises are not taught to children as they may cause harm. The following is performed by an experienced young man. Please remember it is important to build up exercises slowly for maximum benefit.

WARM-UP 1 – *Leg stretch to strengthen inner thighs.*

△ From a standing position, bend your front (left) leg at an angle of about 90 degrees, while keeping your rear (right) leg straight. Push forwards to stretch your inner thigh. Repeat this exercise with your right leg forwards. Hold the tension for 5–10 seconds, change to your left leg and repeat the exercise 3–4 times.

WARM-UP 2 – *The splits are excellent for stretching your inner thighs.*

❶ △ With legs astride, gently lower your body as far as you can. It may take some months before you can fully reach the floor. Only go as wide as you comfortably can and practice on a regular basis to improve your suppleness in this exercise.

❷ △ The ultimate aim of this exercise is to be able to lower your head down to touch the floor. This increases the pressure on the inner thighs. Lean forwards, pushing your head down as far as you comfortably can.

WARM-UP 3 – *Press-ups assist in developing the top part of the body.*

△ With the palm of your hands down, feet together and body straight, gently lower your body to the floor. Do not touch the floor but keep your body elevated about 1–2 inches (2.5-5 cm). Push back up to the starting position and repeat. Breathe out as you lower your body, and in as you push back up. *Caution: only perform this exercise 2–3 times and build up gradually. Children under 11 should not perform this exercise, except for a modified version, on knees, and under qualified supervision.*

WARM-UP 4 – *Back and leg stretch for suppleness.*

△ Lower your body so that you can place your right leg to the side and your left knee facing forward at a 90 degree angle. Take hold of your right ankle with your right hand and lower your head towards your right knee. Keep your leg straight for maximum stretch. Do not be concerned if you cannot touch your knee in the early stages, as this will come with practice. Only lower yourself to a position that feels comfortable, pushing a little further each time. Change to the left leg and repeat the exercise 3 times each side.

Technique | Children's self-defence

Shinto ryu seeks to develop all our senses, capabilities and skills to the maximum, and arm us to deal with any difficult situation wisely and safely. While it may be perceived that only the fit and young can practise a martial art, rudimentary skills can be applied to a defence situation by all ages, gender and abilities.

DEFENCE 1 *Children can apply the power of the circle very effectively to disengage an attack.*

❶ ◁ The attacker makes a double-handed grab, pulling you off the ground.

❷ △ Take hold of the aggressor's thumbs with both hands.

❸ △ Using an outwards circular motion, pull the aggressor's thumbs down. This will cause pain and encourage the aggressor to let go and allow you to escape.

DEFENCE 2 – *This demonstrates how children can use their strengths against an aggressor's weaknesses.*

❶ △ The aggressor moves in with a single-handed grab to your body.

❷ ▷ Step back to create distance and bring the knife edge of your right hand up in a semi-circular motion to deflect the grab. Slide your hand down towards the aggressor's hand and take hold of his wrist or, if you have a small hand, as much of his hand as you can take hold of. It is important to keep this as a continuous action, since it is the momentum and the body movement which enhance the success of the technique.

△ Even though you may have a small hand, taking hold of the aggressor's little fingers and using the power of the circle, can assist in breaking a grip.

❸ ▷ As you continue the circular action with your right hand, bring your left hand up under the aggressor's right elbow to assist the action. If you find this difficult, as the aggressor is moved downwards, bring your forearm across his elbow and your body forward, keeping the momentum and control towards the floor. From this position either throw away, as you have prevented the grab, or continue to restrain, depending on the situation.

△ As the circular action continues, the aggressor's palm should turn upwards so that pressure can then be applied to the elbow.

❹ △ Keep applying pressure by rotating the hold, which, in turn, will assist in pushing the aggressor to the floor. Keep your body weight over the elbow joint to secure the pressure. Call for assistance or leave the area.

❶ △ An aggressor moves in and grabs your hair with the intention of pulling you back and off balance.

❷ △ Bring both your hands up above your head. Remain upright or slightly lower your position, depending upon the size of the aggressor. Either way, it is important not to lean back.

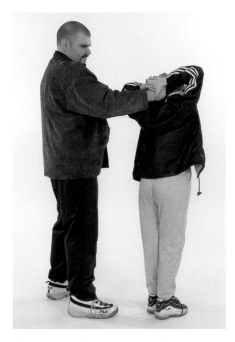

❸ △ Place both hands on top of your head and lock your fingers together. Push down firmly to apply a locking technique on the aggressor's hand. This will minimize the pain of having your hair pulled and start the disengagement. If you have small hands, attempt to find the most comfortable grip for you, ensuring your fingers are securely locked together, and press down. As you turn, you may find your hands starting to grip the wrist. This is acceptable if it assists in maintaining control by turning the aggressor's arm.

❹ △ Continue to turn your body in towards the aggressor, maintaining a firm grip.

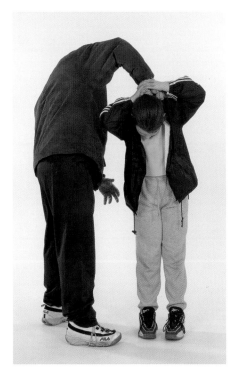

❺ △ As you almost complete your turn you will feel his grip start to loosen. Be aware of his other arm and legs at all times, in the event he may try to strike. *Note: the faster you apply this turn, the easier it is to encourage him to let go, through the pain inflicted on his joints, tendons and muscles.*

❻ △ At the end of the turn, the aggressor should have released your hair. To maintain control bring your thumbs around on to the top of the aggressor's hand. Apply pressure with the thumbs in a forwards and downwards motion. Then, either push the aggressor away or apply a "hard" technique, such as a kick to the solar plexus or face (depending upon the seriousness of the attack). If you are in an isolated area you may need to apply a hard technique to incapacitate the aggressor for a long period of time. A unique aspect of shinto ryu is the fact that, whilst training occurs within the traditional environment, emphasis is also placed on training in various surroundings e.g. in parks, the street, home or work. In other words, it is applicable in everyday situations and in everyday clothes.

Technique | Women's self-defence

Women's self-defence features strongly in shinto ryu, with its modern outlook. Handling more than one aggressor at the same time may be viewed as an impossible task, but it is important to apply a strategy that utilises your strength to maximum effect against an aggressor's weaknesses, so that you can safely escape from a difficult situation.

CAUTION

As an initial strategy, it is always best to avoid conflict by applying such skills as verbally de-fusing the situation, body language and similar strategies. If this does not work, only then, as a last resort, apply physical self-defence, using "reasonable force" to protect yourself (or others). Even if you successfully defend yourself, an aggressor may have the right to sue you. The law varies from country to country and you may be called on to prove that reasonable force only was used. It is, therefore, preferable to use restraining techniques, depending upon the seriousness of the situation.

❶ △ One of the aggressors grabs your wrist with his right hand. If you have an item such as an umbrella, make use of this in your defence. Apply a circular action with your wrist (the same technique used with or without an umbrella) to disengage the grab.

❷ △ If you do have an umbrella to aid your defence, twist to position it over the aggressor's wrist. Bring your left hand underneath and take hold of the umbrella to lock the aggressor's wrist. Push down to apply pressure and take the aggressor to the floor.

❸ △ Usually, if you successfully disengage the first aggressor, other aggressors can be dissuaded from continuing with the assault. Where this is not the case, apply the power of the circle to disengage the grab and strike to a weak point, such as the face or throat. *Caution: this is the last-resort application, when all else has failed, and when you believe your life is in imminent danger. When practising with a partner, focus (aim) your technique – do not make contact.*

❹ △ Strike to the vulnerable area, such as the throat. *Caution: this is an extremely dangerous area to strike and should only be used as a last resort in a serious situation.*

Technique | Disengagement

Being grabbed about your body, wrist, arm, shoulder or clothing is another type of assault. Ideally, always try to talk your way out of the situation and keep a safe distance between you and the aggressor. However, if an aggressor moves in to grab you, it is important to try to disengage the grip before you are physically struck.

BODY GRAB – *Defence against a body grab.*

❶ ◁ An aggressor makes a grab with his right hand to your left lapel.

❷ ◁ Place your left hand completely over the aggressor's right hand, aiming to lock his thumb and fingers. Keep close to your chest for maximum control and start to pull outwards to cause the aggressor to release his grip. At the same time, depending upon the circumstances, strike to the nose. This will cause the eyes to water which, in turn, will obscure the aggressor's vision and give you a chance to escape.

❸ ◁ Following the strike, bring your right hand under the aggressor's right arm and take hold of his right hand. You are now preparing to throw the aggressor to the floor.

△ Close-up of both hands gripping the aggressor's right hand in preparation to throw.

❹ △ Continue the momentum of the arm movement forward, while at the same time stepping through. You need to ensure you are very close to the aggressor to break his posture and balance. Remember that these techniques are successful only when applied with correct timing, skill and body movement.

REAR DEFENCE – *Defence against a grab from the rear.*

1 △ As the aggressor grabs you with his right arm around your throat from the rear, immediately try to drop your chin downwards, to alleviate any pressure against your throat. At the same time, turn your body inwards towards the aggressor and aim to take hold of thumb and fingers.

2 △ Pull the aggressor's arm forwards, locking his elbow on top of your right shoulder. Ensure that you push the aggressor's palm outwards, with his fingers pointing downwards for maximum effect. Keep your body upright to maintain pressure on his elbow joint.

3 △ Using a circular motion, bring the aggressor's arm around your right side, preparing to throw him. Although a smaller child may find this throw awkward to execute, it should present little difficulty for a teenager or adult.

4 ▷ The aggressor will be winded, or at least disorientated, as he lands on the floor. This will incapacitate him, allowing you time to escape. If there is any possibility that the attacker could still be a threat, strike with a leg technique of your choice.
Note: remember the law and the use of "reasonable force". It is always best to incapacitate the aggressor with minimum force and get away to safety. However, depending upon the circumstances, you may have no alternative but to follow through with a further technique, to ensure you have enough time to escape.

5 △ Continue to maintain an assertive attitude because, in spite of being floored, the aggressor could try to retaliate (or there may be other assailants close by). You may have been successful in your defensive manoeuvre, but don't be overconfident. Keep alert until you are safely out of the situation.

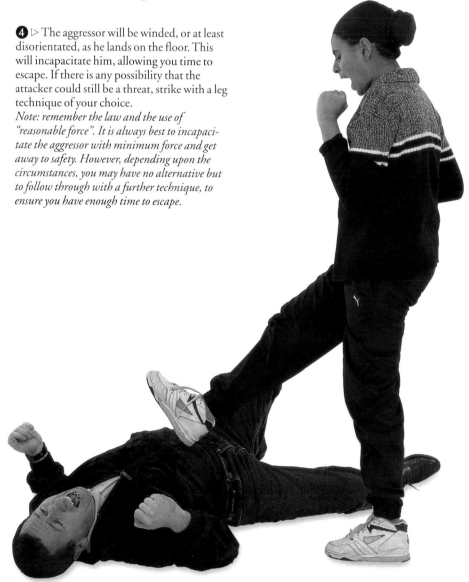

Technique | Knife defence

While a knife attack is unlikely, being prepared builds self-confidence. Shinto ryu encourages students to practise defence moves against weapons to ensure that people have the ability to defend and disarm should the need arise. However, the fundamental principle of defence should always be to verbally defuse the situation, if possible.

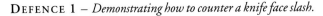

DEFENCE 1 – *Demonstrating how to counter a knife face slash.*

❶△ A slashing knife attack is very frightening, but as the aggressor comes in, duck down to avoid the knife.

❷△ As the knife swings back round, bring your body up and block the aggressor's right arm with the edge of your right hand or forearm. Ensure you turn your body away from the knife attack as you block. Remember it is not the knife that is dangerous but the person using it!

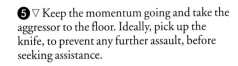

❺ ▽ Keep the momentum going and take the aggressor to the floor. Ideally, pick up the knife, to prevent any further assault, before seeking assistance.

❸△ Twist completely around inwards, towards the aggressor, leading with your left foot. Spin your body clockwise so that you are facing the same way as the aggressor. Keep the knife away from you by bringing your left arm over the attacker's right arm, ideally aiming for just above the elbow joint, and take hold of your own right wrist. Apply pressure by locking your arms. Keep your body close to the side of the aggressor to maintain maximum control.

❹△ Pivot on both feet, turning in an anti-clockwise (counterclockwise) direction to face the aggressor. At the same time, apply a circular action to the aggressor's wrist, bending his elbow so that the knife ends up behind the aggressor. This continuous, flowing movement will cause pain, and should encourage the aggressor to drop the knife.

DEFENCE 2 – *Demonstrating how to defend against a knife body lunge.*

❶ ◁ An aggressor moves in with a knife attack to the stomach. Side step the attack and block with your left arm, taking hold of the left wrist to stop the knife attack. This technique is one of many knife defences used in shinto ryu.

❷ ▷ Place your left arm under the aggressor's elbow joint, and take hold of his right wrist with your right hand, to apply an elbow lock to release the knife.

❸ ◁ If the aggressor has not already dropped the knife, this is the time to apply further pressure to release the weapon. Pin the aggressor's arm against your chest to apply pressure against the elbow joint, keeping the knife away from your body. Simultaneously move in and strike the hinge of his mandible (jaw bone close to the lower ear) with your left elbow. Remember, if the aggressor came in with a left-hand knife attack, you would apply the above from the opposite side.

biographies

BIOGRAPHIES

252

BIOGRAPHIES

TAE KWONDO
Ron Sergiew

Ron Sergiew started training in tae kwondo in 1972 and gained his black belt in 1976. He is currently 5th-*dan*.

Ron's competition career started in 1973 and spanned 16 years, during which he became British Champion on numerous occasions, and ultimately World and European Champion. Ron became a professional instructor in 1980, and since that time has produced many black belts. While teaching full time, he still managed to become involved in the founding of the Tae Kwon-Do Association of Great Britain, which is now the largest UK tae kwondo organization.

His responsibilities within that organization are: National Treasurer, Grading Examiner for coloured belt and black belt testings and North Midlands area representative.

WADO RYU
Eugene Alexander Codrington

Eugene Codrington's competition career began in 1974 when he became the AKA Champion. He is currently 6th-*dan* and has achieved over 30 national and international titles on an individual and team basis, including five times British Champion, twice European All Styles individual and team champion and World Team Champion 1975. He founded his own karate organization in 1986, The Codrington European Karate-Do Development Organization.

He is a national referee for the English karate governing body and head of the delegation for the national squad.

SHOTOKAN
Father Seamus Mulholland OFM

Seamus Mulholland is a 6th-*dan shihan*, shotokan karate; 6th-*dan* daisho-kenshi mu te katsu ryu takamura batto jutsu; and 3rd-*dan* katakori jo do. He is an exponent of tessan shon-to (Japanese fan) and a specialist in kata oyo (close quarter combat). He is currently Chief Instructor at Newham Shotokan Karate Kai.

He is the author of *Traditional Karate* and has written for various magazines.

AIKIDO
Peter Brady

Peter Brady is a 5th-*dan* - so-hombu, B.A.B. Senior Coach.

He first practised aikido in 1969. In 1972 he became affiliated to the Aikikai of Great Britain through the West Midlands Aikikai. He also assisted in establishing the East Birmingham Hospital Dojo, practising and teaching there until 1980.

He has had extensive experience – training with nearly every Hombu Shihan that has taught in England, including Dorshu Kisshomaru Ueshira, Saito Sensei, Tamura Sensei, Yamaguchi Sensei and Chiba Sensei, to name but a few.

He currently holds the position of *shodan* of the United Kingdom Aikikai (Senior Instructor) and is responsible for five clubs throughout the country.

JU-JITSU
Kevin Pell Shihan

Kevin Pell Shihan, 6th-*dan*, has over 27 years' experience in martial arts. He is the founder and Chief Instructor at Ishin Ryu Ju-Jitsu Renmei, whose headquarters are in Hertfordshire.

Ishin ryu ju-jitsu is the culmination of Pell Shihan's experience in the arts of ju-jitsu, karate, shorinji kempo and Chinese boxing. He is an Executive Officer and joint founder of the United Alliance of Independent Martial Artists and is in the process of setting up *dojo*s in Israel, Denmark, Zimbabwe and Spain.

JUDO
Neil Adams MBE

Neil Adams' personal achievements are judo 7th-*dan*, World Judo Champion, 1981; Silver Medal, 1980 Moscow Olympic Games; Silver Medal, 1984 Los Angeles Olympic Games; seven times European Champion; 19 times British Champion (Junior and Senior); Olympic Judo Team Coach; 1996 Atlanta Olympic Games and British Schools Judo Association Coach, 1989–1997.

He is the author of several books, including: *A Life in Judo*, *Olympic Judo Throwing Techniques*, *Olympic Judo Preparation Training* and the *Judo Masterclass Series*.

He is currently employed by the British Judo Association as Technical Coach, and also runs a full-time judo centre and Health and Fitness Club in Coventry.

WING CHUN
James Sinclair

James Sinclair began martial arts training in 1972. He founded the UK Wing Chun Kung Fu Association in 1985 and graduated from the British School of Shiatsu-Do (London) in 1994. He is known as the teacher's teacher, due to the well-respected instructors he has produced.

Master James Sinclair has conducted seminars and demonstrations with many of the elite martial artists of the world, such as Dan Inosanto (JKD & Kali), Master Sken (Thai Boxing), Greg Wallace (6th-*dan* BASKA), Kevin Brewerton (World Semi-Contact Champion), Bob Fermor (Nunchaku and other weapons), Mike Billman (5th-*dan* shotokan karate), Terry Coughtrey (3rd-*dan* ju-jitsu) and Dave Oliver (tae kwondo 6th degree).

MOK-GAR
Paul J Boyer

Paul Boyer started his martial arts training in 1974. In 1976, he was introduced to Master Charles Chan, who taught traditional Shaolin mok-gar kuen kung fu.

He is experienced in numerous weaponry and the internal tai chi wu style of tai chi chuan. He obtained his black sash in 1979 and opened a club at the Norman Green sports centre, where he still practises the style of traditional Shaolin mok-gar kuen kung fu.

Additionally, he is a lecturer in sports injuries and complementary therapies.

KICK BOXING
Elaine Adani

Elaine Adani began martial arts training in 1985 with lau gar kung fu, under an instructor from Birmingham called Steve Faulkner. By 1988 she had achieved Green Sash status and had started to be interested in the sporting aspects of martial arts training, and moved over to kick boxing with a lau gar affiliated club in Leicester.

Since 1986 she has been to many tourna-

ments throughout the UK and has held a world title as well as a British title.

She trains with the Leicester Pirates and has been successful in encouraging more women to take up the sport, after initially being the only woman member. As a senior at the club, she coaches, instructs and takes gradings.

TAI CHI
Robert Poyton

Robert Poyton began training in traditional Yang Family tai chi chuan in the early 1980s. He is Chief Instructor of the San Chai Tai Chi Academy, which runs classes, residential courses and regular workshops, both in the UK and abroad. Robert has written for numerous publications and is Editor of *Tai Chi International*, the UK's leading tai chi art magazine.

KENDO/IAIDO
Trevor Jones

Trevor Jones is a 6th-*dan* iaido, kendo 4th-*dan*, judo 1st-*dan*. He has been studying kendo and iaido for 20 years, including several years in Japan, and has represented Great Britain in European and World Championships for kendo. He currently teaches in London and is a former British Kendo Champion.

KENDO
Hiroshi Sugawara

Hiroshi Sugawara is 5th-*dan* kendo. He studied kendo in Miyagi Prefecture, Japan, for 20 years and in Hokkaido, Japan, for 10 years.

KENDO
Derek Raybold

Derek Raybold started in the art of kendo in 1976, forming the Birmingham Kendo Club in 1978. He is currently 4th-*dan* kendo and 2nd-*dan* aikido. He has been a member of the British Kendo Squad for five years and represented Great Britain in the 1985 World Kendo Championships in Paris.

IAIDO
Fay Goodman

Fay Goodman is internationally qualified to a high level in many martial arts. She is a leading exponent of shinto ryu (8th-*dan* – combination of karate, aikido and ju-jitsu) and iaido (6th-*dan*), winning the gold medal in the 1995 European Championships. She is widely respected as one of the highest graded female martial artists in the world. As a coach with the British Kendo Association and other international bodies, she represents various martial arts. Fay is a highly qualified personal safety consultant and, as a journalist and TV personality, contributes on a variety of business and social issues. Previous books include *Self-Defence for All*, *Beating Crime in your Business* and *Be Streetwise*. She has produced a TV documentary series on martial arts, to which the soundtrack, *"Koroko – Spirit of the Heart"*, is available.

SHINTO RYU
Clive Preece

Clive Preece has been involved with martial arts since 1968. He is the founder and Councillor of the European Martial Arts Academy, Chief Director of Junior Defence -Line, 8th-*dan* European Martial Arts Academy, 8th-*dan* shinto ryu, *dan*-graded judo, aikido, shukokai and shotokan.

Since 1985 he has been teaching self-defence and confidence building to children from 3½ to 16 years of age.

index

254

INDEX

ACKNOWLEDGEMENTS
I would like to say a special thank you to my family, friends, fellow practitioners and work colleagues who have supported me in the writing of this publication. The days and nights of burning the midnight oil, working over the festive season and New Year was only achieved by the support and dedication of many people.

I have enjoyed writing this book, even though it was hard work. It is one of those projects I have wanted to write for many years. As they say, patience is a virtue, and when the time is right the door will open (a gentle opening would have been preferred to the force of a tornado!).

So as we journey through life we all have different paths to follow. I travel this path with the ultimate aim of giving those I meet the true kindness and sincerity which has been shown to me by very special people, during my years as a martial arts practitioner and teacher. I have learnt so much, but I have so much more to learn. In the words of a famous quote:

Be firm in your acts, but easy in your heart; be strict with yourself; but be gentle with your fellow men

Tut Tut

This book would not have come to fruition without the loyal support and help from other people for which I am most grateful. The collection of material, guidance and contributions of certain individuals is gratefully acknowledged below:
Clive Preece and his team, Derek Creedon, Derek Raybold, Elaine Adani and Kevin McClennahon, Eugene Codrington and his team, Father Seamus Mulholland (bless him) and Juliette, Graham Kenning, Hiroshi Sugawara, James Sinclair (for persevering with his e-mail contributions) and his team, Kerstie Hodrien for many hours or typing, Kerry Elkins for support in typing the publication, Kevin Pell and Miguel Camacho (for superb painting skills and burning the midnight oil with a maze of photographs), Mark Wolski for burning the midnight oil proofreading, Neil Adams and his team, Paul Boyer and Chris Goodburn, Peter Brady (for your tremendous patience) and Cath Davies, Ron Sergiew and his team, Roy Preece (my father, for his courage) and family, Robert Poyton and his team, Trevor Jones, the British Kendo Association, Lingus Dignam, and Mark Peters of Kai Ming Martial Arts Association for kindly making his *dojo* available in the Tai Chi section.

A special thank you to David Mills of CIMAC for contributing some of the clothing and equipment in the different sections – thank you.
And to my teachers for their generous and kind teachings over the years: Haruna Matsuo Sensei, Ishido Shizufumi Sensei, Oshita Masakazu Sensei, Fujii Okimitsu Sensei, Fukura Sensei, Ide Sensei, Chiba Sensei, Kanetsuka Sensei, Hirori Sensei, Eddie Daniels, A Hunt and T Foster.
And to all those other teachers and friends with whom I have practised and shared so much over the years – too many to name. The poem on page 4 is dedicated to you all with my sincere gratitude and thanks.
Fay Goodman

FOR GENERAL INFORMATION OR ENQUIRIES REGARDING MARTIAL ARTS:
contact Goodman Multimedia on (+44) 0121 784 8268
or email at: goodmanmultimedia@eclipse.co.uk

MODEL ACKNOWLEDGEMENTS:
tae kwondo: Fiona Newcomb, Terry Read, Stuart Penn, Carole Gameson, Lorraine Oliver, Dale Newcomb *wado ryu:* Simon Walker *shotokan:* Juliette Littlewood *aikido:* Cath Davies *ju-jitsu:* Miguel Camacho *judo:* Ceri Richards, Emma George, Andy Smith, Ashley Adams *wing chun:* Sifu Mark Phillips, Jacob Jaywant, Nathan Jaywant, Joshua Jaywant, William Jaywant, Avril Kinsley, Deborah Smith *mok-gar kuen:* Chris Goodburn *kick boxing:* Rachael Barton, Kevin McClennahon *tai chi chuan:* Steve Blatchet, Kathy Chi, Robert Poynton *shinto ryu:* Derek Creedon, Ava Preece, Sophie Preece, Veera Kaur, Jevanpal Singh Choudhary, Mark Fisher, Paul Yeomans, Neil Smith. (Jagman Singh and Amar Kaur Choudhary, Harpaal and Harbinder Kaur – thank you for your time).
PICTURE CREDITS – Additional pictures supplied by:
Hulton Getty: p6, p28 top, p31 top, p98, p100 left, p130, p212
Tony Stone: p7 top, p8 top, p9 both, p27, p29, p67, p99, p131 top, p179, p195 both.
Simon Lailey: p7 bottom, p8 bottom, p13, p26, p28 bottom, p30, p50, p51 both, p146, p147 both, p148-9, p162, p163 both, p164, p178 top, p210, p229 both.
Tai Chi International: p194, p196 top
Fay Goodman: p226–8.
e.t. archive: p67, p99.
Werner Forman Archive: p211.